Myles Horton Father Of The Civil Rights Movement

MYLES TO GO

by
SPENCER GRIN and ASHER HEY

Copyright © 2020 by Spencer Grin and Asher Hey.

ISBN:	Hardcover	978-1-6641-3738-7
	Softcover	978-1-6641-3737-0
	eBook	978-1-6641-3736-3

All rights reserved. No part of this book may be reproduced or transmitted in any form or by any means, electronic or mechanical, including photocopying, recording, or by any information storage and retrieval system, without permission in writing from the copyright owner.

The views expressed in this work are solely those of the author and do not necessarily reflect the views of the publisher, and the publisher hereby disclaims any responsibility for them.

Any people depicted in stock imagery provided by Getty Images are models, and such images are being used for illustrative purposes only.
Certain stock imagery © Getty Images.

Cover Photo: MYLES HORTON

Print information available on the last page.

Rev. date: 11/06/2020

To order additional copies of this book, contact:
Xlibris
844-714-8691
www.Xlibris.com
Orders@Xlibris.com
819545

CONTENTS

DEDICATION i
PREFACE 1
I.   BREAKING THE MOLD 5
II.   COLLEGE AWAKENING 11
III. THE BIRTH OF AN IDEA 18
IV. WHY DENMARK 28
V.   THE HIGHLANDER SCHOOL 34
VI. DEATH THREATS 48
VII. STATE OF TENNESSEE V. HIGHLANDER 54
VIII. PALENQUE: BIRTHPLACE OF FREEDOM FROM SLAVERY 61
IX. COURAGEOUS ROSA PARKS 68
X.   FATHER OF THE CIVIL RIGHTS MOVEMENT & THE TIMELINE 77
XI. KINDRED SPIRIT FROM BRAZIL 86
XII. MYLES LEGACY: MILES TO GO 94
XIII. THE PATH 98
XIV. MYLES TO GO 115

SOURCES 117
ABOUT THE AUTHORS 119

DEDICATION

THIS BOOK IS dedicated to our lovely and loving family, each of whom deeply believe in the dignity and equality of all people,

and

wish that all the people on this planet would unite to protect the earth and save our planet from foolhardy environmental, and nuclear destruction.

PREFACE

ROSA PARKS IN 1955's segregated Alabama refused to give up her seat in front of the bus which was the spark that ignited THE CIVIL RIGHTS MOVEMENT IN THE UNITED STATES.

Later Martin Luther King expressed his hope for a country still refusing to recognize the equality of all men and women. His famous "I HAVE A DREAM" speech recited in front of one quarter million people at the Washington, D.C. mall summarized the quest for an end to racism in the United States. This is the true meaning of democracy, and the truly moral creed "that all men are created equal".

Where did Martin Luther King's dream originate? What motivated Rosa Parks' dignified protest to refuse to move to the back of the bus?

Both Reverend King and Mrs. Parks were students of Myles Horton, who many decades earlier imagined a world where whites and blacks could live, work, and learn together. Today, he is considered the Father of the Civil Rights Movement in the United States.

Part of this book is the story of the amazing Highlander School that he founded in the segregated South in 1932 which had white and black people studying side by side from the day it opened its doors. His defiance and violation of laws promoting segregation produced death threats and murder, not only by white supremacist organizations like the Ku Klux Klan, but through government action as well.

Southern states at the time had passed laws protecting their rights to segregation and white superiority. There are many many examples of lynching, murder and threats to maintain the status quo in the South. Even though they are not the most horrific, we have chosen to give the following two examples to show just how diverse the attempts were to silence those who opposed segregation.

One example is the unwanted hysterectomy of Fannie Lou Hamer performed without her consent. She was a black student at Highlander, and founder of the Mississippi Freedom Party. Forcing her to have this horrible procedure was one way Mississippi was attempting to reduce the black population and suppress the "black vote".

Another example was the state of Tennessee, threatened by the anti-segregation practices and activism at the Highlander School, sued Highlander on trumped up charges. As a result of the lawsuit's success in court; the school was actually closed.

Undaunted, the school reopened the very next day, and Myles Horton continued his civil disobedience fighting for what was right.

In addition to Rosa Parks, Martin Luther King, and Fannie Lou Hamer, the Highlander School had many illustrious alumnae who fought for equality including Andrew Young, a leader of the Southern Christian Leadership Conference, Stokley Carmichael of the Student Nonviolent Coordinating Committee, Ralph Bunch, the United Nations Ambassador, Julian Bond, the United States Senator, and Eleanor Roosevelt, a First Lady and wife of President Franklin Roosevelt.

What is especially amazing is that Myles Horton was white and poor. He was born on July 9, 1905 in a rural hamlet of Savannah, Georgia.

The force of his own free will, opposition to unjust laws, determination, and great courage led him to college, and then to international travel which opened his eyes to ideas that challenged the status quo, and ultimately was the catalyst for the civil rights movement in the U.S.A.

How did it happen that a boy, born in poverty into a family with no formal education, rose to become the teacher, mentor, and inspiration for future civil rights leaders, giving them courage, dignity, and values which included a sense of justice, equality and respect?

It is why Dr. Morris Mitchell, the Southern educator, who also like Myles studied under the distinguished Columbia University Professor, John Dewey, called Myles Horton,

"The Father of the Civil Rights Movement".

Indeed it was Horton who planted the seeds for Rosa Parks to spark the civil rights movement, and for the Reverend Martin Luther King to lead his non- violent march for equality, dignity, and an end to segregation.

These, however, were not the only seeds Myles Horton planted which took root and spread widely. He was the first to help labor organize in the South, and fight exploitation. He was first to let a young black woman who did not have a high school education become a teacher and lead the movement to teach literacy. This outreach spawned large numbers of "citizenship schools" and taught thousands in the South to read, write, and vote.

Myles Horton was the educator who early on championed experiential learning, He also led a nonviolent protest against segregation, labor exploitation, and other ills of society. By his own non- violent example, along with his wife who popularized the song *We Shall Overcome*, and other colleagues, and students, he blazed a path for a more equal and humane society. These values, embraced by his beloved Highlander School which he founded in rural Appalachia, has continued to operate for over 85 years to the present day.

I

BREAKING THE MOLD

FOR MYLES HORTON, a child born at the turn of the last century in the segregated deep Southern impoverished part of the United States of America, the mold was broken. One can liken it to the metamorphosis of a butterfly. From an earthbound caterpillar it becomes a beautiful butterfly with wings which enable it to soar into the sky.

So it was with the little boy, named Myles, who was able to break the mold, and develop ideas and examples in living and education that were so new that they soared, and remain in existence to this very day.

Myles Horton, like many in the hills of rural Tennessee in the early 1900's in Cumberland Valley, Appalachia, was born into a hard working poor family who had no access to formal education. His grandparents were illiterate, and his parents worked as sharecroppers unable to break free from the cycles of poverty. No matter what they did, it was for very low wages, and they could not break out of the desolation of being extremely poor.

It all started from a very humble beginning. Some bigoted people referred to the Horton family as "white trash' because they were poor and had little formal education. Such an intolerant description was not only inaccurate, but very misleading. True in the hills of rural Tennessee in the early 1900's in Cumberland Valley in Appalachia, the population consisted mainly of hard working poor families who mainly had no formal education, and labored for very meager wages as sharecroppers on farms, workers in saw mills, factories, and mines.

Although poor in material wealth, Myles Horton's father, Perry Horton, and mother Elsie Falls Horton, were rich in the Christian values of "treat your neighbor as you would want him to treat you".

They both had limited access to education, but were literate. Both had only gone to grammar school; but understood and appreciated the value of a good education. As a matter of fact they both became teachers. At that time and place you did not have to go to school or have credentials to become a teacher. Later they had to give up that noble calling when licenses became required for teachers.

Myles, born on July 9,1905 was the eldest of four children. Perry and Elsie Horton were honest loving parents who took their children, Pearl, Dan, Delmas, and Myles to the Cumberland Presbyterian Church to which they belonged. They taught right from wrong. His mother held bible classes. His parents also knew the value of hard work. During his life Perry Horton worked as a town clerk, and also in factories, and on the farm as a sharecropper.

Although the Hortons never attended High School their interest in education was quite evident. They understood that although their grandfather was an illiterate "mountain man" who had never gone to any school and could not read; he was a smart man. He bought and sold cattle; and when it came to prices he would do the arithmetic in his head, and always came up with the right answers. When asked about schooling he said "never thought about it; there were no schools near where we lived".

However, both Elsie and Perry valued a good education. One time, after Myles had already started college, the family decided to move. Before they decided where they would settle, his father wrote letters to five counties inquiring about the school system. He wanted Myle's sister, Elsie, and two younger brothers, Dan and Delmas, to have a good high school education. As a matter of fact he did move to one of the five counties with the best high school, even though he did not have a job at that location. Sometime later his parents who missed Myles, decided to move to where he was going to school. They settled in at Forkadeer River Valley, the community where the High School was located, and so the whole family was reunited.

Myles played on the football team of his high school, and learned how good strategy can affect the outcome of the game. It was a lesson he never forgot as he developed a strategy for his Highlander School….. the school he founded which defied the laws of segregation.

Growing up Myles Horton learned the value of service to the community. Although it meant that some of the family meals were quite meager; his mother would share food with those who were less fortunate. She was a good hearted soul who was a true christian in her values. Not in the formal trappings of the church, but in doing good deeds for her fellow men and women. She helped many young women during their pregnancies. She also helped to feed their very large families even though it meant depriving her own family of some food.

Way back then she was telling her neighbors about birth control; a very unpopular position which she readily espoused. She taught Myles to think for himself. For example once when he said to his mother that he did not believe the doctrine of predestination of the Presbyterian church his mother said, "That's just the preacher's talk; don't bother about that. Just believe that you should love your neighbor; that's all it is about".

The church the family attended was rational rather than revivalist. It placed emphasis on good works in this world, rather than on salvation in the next. This is what Elsie Horton believed and taught her son. This is the doctrine she practiced every day, which had a strong impact on the young mind of Myles Horton.

The issue of the very low wages did not surface for Myles until the age of 15. At that age while going to school he worked in a saw mill. The work in the mill was for a meager wage and was quite dangerous, and there were many severe accidents that took place there. Myles immediately knew how badly the workers were underpaid; but was still too young to do much about it.

Later he got a job making crates to house tomatoes for shipment. He and the workers were paid a half penny a crate, and no matter how fast one worked, the weekly wage was not nearly enough to get by. He quickly noticed that those workers who put in the final nails to close the crate were paid more than he and those who built the crates. It was his first experience in organizing, and it came out of necessity. He and his co-workers asked for a raise. They were refused.

Myles figured that if there were no workers to build the crates, that when more tomatoes arrived from the local farms they would soon become rotten, and so he organized the other workers to threaten to quit if their demands were not met.

> The bosses said, "okay; if you quit we will get other workers to build the crates".

Myles Horton, although only a high school student, had done his homework carefully and thoroughly. He had canvassed the local communities. He knew that there was not a sufficient supply of workers who could come to work quickly, and build crates fast enough to accommodate the large flow of tomatoes from the local farmers. He and his co-workers quit their jobs. It only took two hours for the bosses to capitulate and grant the raises. So in 1922 it was Myles first attempt at organizing, and it was successful.

A few years later Myles got a job in a factory making baskets to house strawberries. Soon he was turning out baskets about ten times as fast as his coworkers. He was told "slow down; work at the same pace the rest of us do. If you work faster you will only replace an existing worker, and you know you will not get paid anymore even though you produce ten times as much". He had invented a system of taking the wood veneer ten pieces at a time, and using the weight of his body to tie them. The foreman came over to him one day and said, "look you can make the baskets as fast as you like; but when you are finished with your output for the day, come up to my office and read so that our total production is the same". He did as he was asked, and spent many hours reading which was his favorite pastime. He also learned what "work control" meant; that is, everyone agreeing to set a daily production goal and not to work any faster. This did not sit well with Myles; but as part of the work force he obeyed the guidelines to which all the other workers adhered.

II

COLLEGE AWAKENING

SOON THE UNTHINKABLE occurred. The church that the Horton family regularly attended encouraged Myles Horton to go to college, and they recommended a small school, Cumberland College in Lebanon, Pennsylvania. Myles and his parents were elated; the first one in the family to even dream of a college education.

During his junior year at Cumberland College, the Presbyterian Church sent Myles Horton to the mountain country of Tennessee to head a vacation bible study program. The town was Ozone, Tennessee with only 350 residents. Myles found the work boring, and he quickly realized that the hymns and prayers had little effect on the everyday real problems and challenges these poor people faced each day in order to get by. The church's educational program he concluded was not meeting the needs of these impoverished communities. He decided to organize meetings in the evenings where the parents of the students could come to discuss and share the problems that they faced. Soon these "community meetings" became crowded. The people discussed many of their problems, such as where can jobs be found, would the trees grow again on the stripped mountain side after the mines were closed, and what about typhoid; how to prevent it?

Although answers to many of the questions were elusive, the populace enjoyed the meetings. There was community singing and camaraderie. Myles was liked so much that he was even offered a free house to become his permanent home; if he would stay on, and not return to college. However, at the time he valued graduating from college, and so did return to Cumberland College.

One of those transformative and unforgettable experiences began in college when Myles became active in the Student YMCA. They were instrumental in pointing out aspects of social and economic injustice, and that segregation was wrong. They had white and black students sit down and discuss the problems of racial inequality. However white and black students could not even share a cup of coffee. Eating together was prohibited. Myles was dismayed that he could not walk into the local public library with a black friend, nor that he could take a Chinese girl into a restaurant.

Myles Horton decided talking was just not good enough; he would act. He organized a dozen chapters in different schools. Nine in white schools and three in black schools. In those days of Jim Crow laws, whites and blacks had to attend separate segregated schools which were all white or all black.

Myles Horton, then 22 years old, spent the summer of 1927 in Ozone, Tennessee organizing Bible Schools for the Presbyterian Church, while at the same time holding meetings where local folk discussed their problems of poverty and racial hatred. They posed questions, many of which were answered, as they shared their own experiences. Some fundamental questions about inequality, however, remained unanswered, and Myles quickly realized he needed more research, study, and experience in order to hopefully help these communities.

After graduating Cumberland College in 1928, Myles Horton took a job as Secretary of all Student YMCAs' in the state of Tennessee. This enabled him to travel, and see the pervasive poverty in many of the communities in the state. He visited many high schools and colleges. He was constantly looking for an education system that would provide answers for the people in Ozone Tennessee, and Appalachia. He could find none that really addressed their problems or ameliorated their conditions.

He then organized a statewide convention of Student YMCA chapters, and sent out lists to each chapter of students who were invited to attend. It was a bold initiative and undertaking. Nothing was said about it being inter-racial, and it was to be held in a hotel in Knoxville, Tennessee. Myles made dinner reservations in the banquet hall; although he knew that blacks would not be served in that hotel. He also arranged for the 120 students who were going to attend to enter the banquet hall to do so directly from the street so that they would not have to go through the hotel.

When the students arrived they all sat down at the tables to eat. The black waiters had never experienced such a gathering before, and approached Myles saying that they could not serve blacks and whites sitting together. Myles knew this was coming, and had a ready answer. "What are you going to do with the food you prepared for 120 people, throw it out...if you do you surely will be fired because we will not pay for food we did not eat". Faced with this dilemma; the waiters relented and did feed everyone. A lesson was learned by all 120 attendees. Action was better than mere words in tackling a problem. If you want to solve a problem you can; if you develop a well thought out action strategy on how to deal with it. People could affect change.

Myles then went to New York where he attended Columbia University Teachers College, the Union Theological Seminary, and then he went to the University of Chicago. While doing graduate work he was greatly influenced by famous professors such as the Columbia University Professor of Education John Dewey.

Dewey's views on education also influenced another Southerner named Morris Mitchell, who also was a graduate student in Professor Dewey's class. He became a great friend of Myles Horton. Morris

Mitchell, the Quaker from Clarksville Georgia, was also a courageous Southerner who opposed segregation. He, too, became an advocate of experiential learning and founded Friends World College; one of the first colleges in the USA to place emphasis and give credit for experiential learning outside of the lecture hall.

Myles Horton made the most of his college years. His quest for a model educational institution to help his neighbors in Tennessee led him to search various religious doctrines, and how they were being practiced. The questions he raised in his mind to reconcile his Christian upbringing and indoctrination with the actual problems of inequality and poverty he saw, made his quest all encompassing. He visited churches of various denominations, jewish temples, muslim mosques, buddhist shrines, all of whom preached the gospel of "love thy neighbor"; but whose hierarchy and members mostly did not actually live and practice that lofty doctrine.

At college he met students from around the world; many with different philosophies. Some were Chinese students who fervently espoused the values of communism. To better understand communism he attended many discussions, and was a frequent visitor to Union Square in New York where communism and socialism were freely discussed. He read the writings of Karl Marx and Lenin. The more he studied, the more he realized that communism was woefully lacking, and that he could never embrace the communist doctrine. However, he was drawn to socialism. He met and supported Norman Thomas who ran for President of the USA on a socialist platform. However, Myles Horton, had concluded early on, that he would accept no label, or permit anyone, or any doctrine, to determine his behavior. He was a free thinker who had to come up with his own conclusions and direction.

Myles did study and come to support the union movement which helped workers organize around a common goal; whether it was to improve their working conditions, or getting a raise in pay so that they could support a family and live a decent life. He quickly realized that there was much to learn, and so continued his education and quest for an education model to help those impoverished neighbors in the mountains of Tennessee.

During a May Day parade, in which Myles participated, a cop hit him on his head with a club yelling " Goddamn Bolshevik". Myles did not understand why he was being hit, or what was meant by the word Bolshevik, so he went back to the Encyclopedia Britannica to find out what the word meant.

This incident also gave rise to a dilemma in Myle's thinking. He had to determine and try to understand whether violence or non-violence was a way to proceed to achieve an objective. Of course the easy answer is non violence; but on closer examination the choice was not always that clear. Two incidents in different parts of the country pointed out the dilemma Myles was facing.

The first such incident was when a black man in Texas was accused of killing a white man. The local mob was ready to take the law into their own hands and lynch him.The National Guard was called out to prevent the lynching. They were on hand, but in a non violent way, refused to do anything to protect the black man. The lynch mob succeeded, and right in front of the National Guard, hung the black man without any intervention by the Guard. The Guard's demeanor was non-violent and lawful; although extremely distasteful. In this case non-violence by the police led to a violent lynching.

The second incident occurred four years later, and it was one in which Myles Horton was personally involved. He was part of a strike called by the United Mine Workers Union in Wilder Tennessee. Barney Graham, a friend of Horton, was President of the local of that union, and death threats were hurled at him. It seemed certain that Graham would be killed, and Myles did everything he could to prevent such a murder. He uncovered the plot to kill Graham, and notified the police; but his information was totally ignored.

Myles' investigation discovered that the men who were hired to kill Graham, were among the same men who had killed eleven people in a labor dispute in Illinois. He unearthed their photographs and names. He supplied these to the local authorities, and even sent a copy to Alva Taylor, a divinity professor at Vanderbilt University whom he admired.

Despite these efforts Graham was murdered!

Myles was present when the issue of Graham's safety was first brought up at the Union meetings. Some said that there was only one way to prevent the thugs from murdering their union leader, and that was to kill them first. There was unanimous agreement that if nothing was done, the murder would take place. Myles agreed; but then presented the problem saying, "If we kill them a war will ensue, and a lot more people will be killed. Would the killing of the two Illinois thugs end the killing?" Myles posed it as a rhetorical question so that it could be debated and a consensus reached.

When Graham was murdered Myles was distraught and dismayed. No one was held responsible. He put the question to clergymen. None could give him an answer. Myles knew, however, that you cannot use force to put or remove ideas in peoples' heads.

III

THE BIRTH OF AN IDEA

ALL THE TIME Myles was searching for a new educational model, he continued to be a voracious reader. One of the books that impressed him greatly was John Dewey's *Reconstruction in Philosophy.* The three volume work of the Pulitzer Prize author, Vernon L. Parrington *Main Currents in American Thought* gave Horton a better understanding of how societies worked. He read *Economic Morality* by Professor Harry F. Ward, and decided to apply to The Union Theological Seminary in New York. He was accepted, and traveled to New York to enroll.

One of the reasons Myles believed that he was accepted was because the Union Theological Seminary wanted a diverse student body which came from all corners of America and comprised ordinary folk. The Union was trying to dispel the perception that they only catered to the wealthy elite. The truth was that most of their students were from the North, and did come from well to do parents. Myles was an exception.

One of the memorable incidents Myles Horton recites is indicative of the type of student the Union attracted. On the day of his arrival, he heard one of the boys ask another person "do you know where I can get a porter to take my luggage to my room". The person being asked was Henry Sloan Coffin, who was then President of the Seminary, and who later became the world renown theologian at Yale University. Coffin picked up the luggage and carried the bags to the dormitory without comment.

The onset of the great depression and the stock market collapse occurred just a few days after Horton's arrival in New York in 1929. All around him people were forming bread lines. The newspapers were reporting almost daily suicides of men who had lost everything. Myles, in dismay, watched closely what was happening in America; while he continued his education.

Myles listened, and was greatly influenced by the lectures of Rheinhold Niebuhr, who had just started teaching at the Union Theological Seminary. Myles became a friend of this eminent Professor. He read his book *Moral Man and Immoral Society* and realized that Niebuhr's allegiance to the idea of socialism had validity. Although it was the friendship and the support of Neibuhr that helped Horton establish the Highlander School; it was the great educator from Columbia University, John Dewey's writings, that formed the underlying philosophy that gave birth to Highlander.

Dewey wrote," It is the aim of education to take part in correcting unfair privilege and unfair deprivation; not to perpetuate them....it must take account of the needs of the existing community life; it must select with the intention of improving life we live in".

This phrase embodied the principle that Horton was beginning to evolve, and which he called the Ozone Project; naming it after the small impoverished community in Tennessee.

A turning point in the project was inspired by two other great teachers, Joseph Hart and Eduard Lindemann. Their writings on adult education indicated that it could be a potent catalyst for social change. Both teachers emphasized the folk schools in Denmark which sparked an immediate interest by Myles Horton. Never before had he encountered teachers and discussions about other places in the world, and what we can learn from them.

Hart wrote, "America is prosperous; beyond the dreams of Denmark in the early nineteenth century where the germ of folk schools first emerged". Lindemann, who was of Danish origin, had studied the role of education in Denmark. The three answers Eduard Lindemann supplied to the theoretical question he asked, resonated with Myles as his thinking on the subject evolved.

The question asked was, "How can education supply directive energy for collective enterprise". The answers Myles thought were provocative and quite revealing.

"1. By revealing the nature of the social process.

2. By transforming the battle of interests from warfare into creative conflict.

3. By developing a method for social functions which will make collective life an educational experience".

Myles started looking and visiting places where he thought such education could flourish. Among the places he visited was Brookwood Labor College which was modeled after Ruskin College in Great Britain. He found that it placed too much emphasis on problems that existed in the cities, and so would not be applicable for rural Tennessee. The visit did produce a surprising result. Myles met another bright student named Elizabeth Hawes who had similar ideas, and impressed Myles Horton. She eventually wound up at the Highlander School as a member of the faculty.

Most of the institutions Myles visited had a bias to what Myles called a "national education". That is, the curriculum was set and imposed on children and adults alike. They had to learn similar subjects in a similar sequence. Much by rote memory. Myles thought that this universal idea of education in America did not grow out of the needs of the people or the community, and certainly could not serve to help the folks he knew in Tennessee.

Myles continued traveling and searching for an institution which embodied his view of an education which was focused on helping people reach their goal toward solving their problems in a meaningful way; and which had a symbiotic relationship among the teachers, staff and local communities.

In his quest he visited settlement houses, and so called utopian communities. Each seemed to fall short of his expectations. Many focused on providing food and shelter for impoverished city folk, and less on solving the underlying problems. Most were located in urban or suburban communities; and so were not applicable for the poor people in Appalachia.

The utopian communities he visited were largely insular. That is they were not part of the community surrounding them. Many of them were struggling with fights about the leadership and direction that their private community should take. Their concerns were narrowly focused on their own problems living in isolation in their own private enclave, and certainly were not adaptable to help the poor mountain people in the South.

Most of the great teachers Myles met in New York were white. He discovered, however, that there were many black people whose ancestors had fled the segregated South for a better life in the North; and that they too had great teachers among them in their community. He realized, however, that he really did not know much about these displaced Southerners. He started reading the writings and poetry of the "blacks". He quickly identified their aspirations as those he admired. Equality for all, freedom for all, and pride in their heritage and leaders. Aside from the life of Dr. DuBois, he was greatly impressed by the poetry of Langston Hughes.

During his stay in New York, Myles became intimately acquainted with Hughes' poem, *I TOO SING AMERICA* whose last lines are, *"Besides they'll see how beautiful I am, and be ashamed. I too am an American"*.

Myles Horton carried all the verses of this Hughes' poem with him on his person, as he traveled looking for the answer to his quest for a relevant education model for his neighbors in Appalachia..

He studied the movement by unions to create better working conditions and pay for workers. He witnessed the deplorable conditions of the "sweat shops" in New York City where garments were made by vastly underpaid workers; some who were under age. He immediately had an emotional attachment to those exploited workers. He also exhibited an intellectual challenge to see if he could help, and so he participated in the International Ladies Garment Workers Union strikes.

He became so committed to fight worker exploitation that he traveled down to Marion, North Carolina where a bitter strike and struggle took place. It has been described as "the first genuinely serious labor revolt the South ever experienced". It arose because of the intolerable working conditions of the workers, and the fact that they were unable to live on the meager pay they were receiving. The strike also revealed the violence and recriminations and penalties imposed on those who dared to oppose their employers. Although this strike was unsuccessful in achieving its purpose, it was the seedling for the labor movement in the South.

Tom Tippett, was a professor that Horton met at the Brookwood Labor College located in a suburb of New York City. This college was founded by a group of trade unionists and educators including John Dewey, the well regarded professor from Columbia University. Tippett was disappointed with what he saw as the impotence of the American Federation of Labor.

While teaching at that college in Katonah, New York, he wrote in his book *When Southern Labor Stirs,* "A labor renaissance is at hand. The American Federation of Labor can take it or leave it alone….Down underneath the Southern unrest is a germ with a will to live, that neither mobs, nor massacres, nor prisons can extinguish".

At the end of one year at New York's Union Theological Seminary, Myles Horton decided that it would be good for him to study under the eminent sociologist Professor Robert Parks who was teaching at the University of Chicago. Myles left New York and went to Chicago. At that time he never seemed interested in graduating or obtaining academic degrees. What he wanted was only to learn and continue his quest for a model educational institution which could help his neighbors in the impoverished South.

Myles left New York in 1930 after witnessing the woes of the depression, and the failure of capitalism to address the issues which caused this catastrophic event in American history. He went to the University of Chicago to further his studies in sociology. He left for Chicago after only one year at the Union Theological Seminary in New York. His focus was not on obtaining more degrees, but rather always was on learning, and on his quest to find an education model that was applicable in rural Tennessee that could help improve the lives of his exploited impoverished neighbors. He thought that studying under the famed sociologist Robert Park would better help him gain insights on how to accomplish his goals.

In Chicago he was indeed greatly influenced by Professor Robert Park at the University of Chicago. While there he also studied at the Chicago Theological Seminary. He never strayed from the true values of Christianity that his parents had taught him, and continued his studies into religions. He sought to find out why the great moral lessons of religion were never really practiced in real life. He also continued to be involved in workers organizing unions to fight for their rights. As a student and member of the Socialist college club; he and some other members of the Club tried to organize the elevator operators at the university. The attempt did not succeed; but it again pointed up a dilemma. Why were not the ideals of the American Federation of Labor actually practiced, so that indeed those elevator operators could get better pay and working conditions?

As always Myles circle of friends extended beyond the confines of the University or the locale in which he was located. One of the most innovative activists he met was Jane Adams, founder of the Hull House in Chicago. Myles wrote, "She put her intelligence to use as well as anyone". He greatly respected her views despite the arguments she presented to him in favor of democracy when he argued in favor of socialism. Adams often quoted Abraham Lincoln in those arguments quoting some of his most famous prose. Lincoln said, "Democracy's most valuable contribution was made to the moral life of the world…in spite of the mistakes, shortcomings and excesses of people".

Adams' life and philosophy made a huge impact on Myles and aided him in formulating his model for the Highlander School which he later developed. She told him, "To arrive at democratic decisions, you need to have a bunch of ordinary people sitting around the stove in a country house or store contribute their own experiences and beliefs; then you take a poll of the majority opinion of those present, regardless of who they are, and that is a democratic decision".

Horton greatly admired Jane Adams' courage. Her views on the futility of war, and rights for women were very unpopular at the time. She did not let threats and intimidation, because of her unpopular positions, ever deter her from her mission. He also admired her open mind. Even though she argued vehemently that democracy was a far better form of government then socialism; she always listened to Myles' ideas, and even once encapsulated the goal that Myles had set for himself. "You really are trying to start a rural settlement house".

Indeed Myles had visited a number of settlement houses while he was in New York, including the Henry Street Settlement House which was focused on helping the poor in the inner city. He thought that the vibrant relationship between the staff and Board at the settlement house and the local community was a very good thing, and something he would try to emulate in his project which he then thought of as the Ozone Project.

In addition to reading and being influenced by Professor Robert Park, Myles also considered himself a "dynamic socialist" because of the book "Dynamic Sociology" written by Dr. Lester Ward. Ward argued that "social progress is only possible through dynamic action", a premise which Horton embraced. He did not entirely agree with Ward's thesis that "poor adults need only the opportunity to learn to take dynamic action". However he entirely agreed with Ward's premise that "poor people have both the will and the appetite to learn; but only lack the means".

A push to visit and study the folk schools in Denmark was provided by a Lutheran Minister who had been born in Denmark and had attended a folk high school there. Myles started to read everything he could about the founding and practice of the folk schools in Denmark. He was intrigued. A great idea of the way Denmark's folk schools operated, mirrored his own thoughts. Although he did not know the language, and Denmark was on another continent, Myles was determined to go there and study there, and see for himself. He practiced what he preached, "experiential learning was a great tool for mastering any subject."

His dream was to start an unconventional school in the mountains of Tennessee to help the impoverished communities, and he thought the "Danish Folk School" model could be the answer he was seeking.

No obstacles would deter him from his quest, and so he did go to Denmark.

IV

WHY DENMARK

IN THE FALL of 1931 Myles Horton arrived in Copenhagen, Denmark. He had arranged living quarters with a family in that city, and immediately started to study Danish at the Borups Folk High School. Simultaneously he started visiting other "folk schools" in Denmark.

He was mostly disappointed because he found that many of the folk schools had strayed far from the principles set out by Bishop Grundtvig, the visionary founder of the Danish Folk Schools.

The Bishop had proposed a "school for life" which was quite radical for the times. It did away with the conventional curriculum, and the requirements to memorize facts. He substituted songs and poetry, and the study of Norse mythology, and he fostered the interaction of teachers and students, and students with other students.

Not only was Myles impressed with the ideas of the 19th century theologian Bishop Grundtvig, but he found him to be a kindred spirit. Both had experienced the woes of an economic depression in their respective countries. Both wanted to give voice to the poor. Both wanted the community to be able to govern themselves without government interference, and both had a common belief in real democracy.

Myles decided that it would be best if he could find older folk schools which had more closely adhered to Bishop Grundtvig's principles, and which helped lead to the cooperative movement in Denmark and to the writing of a democratic constitution. And so his quest continued as he traveled in Denmark observing and learning while trying to master the Danish language. He found success in two older schools, and enrolled as a student. One was the International People's College at Elsinore. The other was the Folk High School For Workers of Esbjerg. Both schools had excellent directors with their own vision of what a folk school should be .

Director Peter Manniche saw the entire planet earth as the campus for his Peoples College. Indeed it inspired another great teacher, Dr. Morris Mitchell, the Quaker from Clarksville, Georgia who was a great friend of Myles Horton. Dr. Mitchell had also studied under John Dewey, and was also interested in founding a new school with emphasis on experiential learning where students could study on different continents. He did so in Long Island, New York where he founded a new college, and named it Friends World College.

It was not easy obtaining accreditation for Friends World College because of the unorthodox curriculum which included experiential learning for which credit was given for work outside the classroom, and also for studying abroad on different continents. At first the Accrediting Board refused to recognize the college,and its unique curriculum. Only after Morris Mitchell sought the advice of an attorney recommended to him, was he able to continue the school's quest for full accreditation. The attorney wrote a brief to present to the Board.

In that successful brief he quoted the exact writing of the Accreditation Board wherein they lauded innovation. He made the argument that in order to achieve innovation some risks had to be taken because this would be new ground without necessarily having a precedent. The most cogent and persuasive argument which convinced the Board to give Friends World College full accreditation was written as follows:

"It is the contention of the Board and faculty of Friends World College that their new form of education and curriculum embracing experiential learning with exposure to diverse peoples and mores of countries on other continents, will result in a real fine liberal arts education which will be equal to, or better than, the conventional college curriculum. It is for this reason that we ask the accrediting body to seriously consider giving Friends World College full accreditation with a provision that if at the end of four years, if their students do not measure up, said accreditation will be removed. The measure could be the results of a test of the freshman class at Friends World College and compare their SAT scores with those of the freshman class of any Ivy League College which usually has the pick of the best and brightest students. Then at the end of four years, again test the same students of both schools with any conventional test and compare the scores".

This argument in the brief proved successful, and Friends World College was accredited with Dr. Morris Mitchell as its President and visionary leader practicing experiential learning for credit toward a regular college degree.

Myles Horton continued his quest in Denmark to find the best example of Danish Folk Schools from which he could adopt and adapt to use in the new school he intended to start when he returned to the USA. Little by little the following set of principles started to emerge in the mind of Dr. Myles Horton which he described to be part of the Ozone Project, the forerunner of the school he wanted to create.

1. Experiential Learning

2. Peer Learning which not only included student to student, but student to teacher and vice versa.

3. Teachers and students living together in a non formal setting comprising all races, religions, ethnicity.

4. Loose organization developed by the teachers and students.

5. Non traditional curriculum developed to help the community ameliorate their condition and live better lives.

6. Freedom from Examinations.

7. Group Singing and Poetry readings.

8. Social interaction among teachers, students and the community.

9. Freedom from state and government regulation.

10. A highly motivating purpose including a way out of poverty.

11. Clarity in what for and what against.

Finally all the elements for the school that Myles envisioned started to take place in his mind. During the holiday period at the year end of 1931, Myles Horton was ready to go back to the USA and start his bold experiment. He wrote:

"I can't sleep, but there are dreams. What you must do is go back, get a simple place, move in and you are there. The situation is there. You start with this and let it grow. You know your goal. It will build its own structure and take its own form. You can go to school all your life, you'll never figure it out, because you are trying to get an answer that can only come from the people in the life situation".

A five year quest had come to an end. It now all seemed so clear to Myles Horton. The way to get started is to start. In his mind he named his project OZONE after the small rural mountain Tennessee community of 350 people which was impoverished because the mines had played out and most of the lumber had already been cut. Myles had visited that community years before he came to Denmark; and now was the time he was returning to the United States to fulfill his dream.

V

THE HIGHLANDER SCHOOL

UPON HIS RETURN to the United States in 1932, all of Myles' energy was focused on making his dream become a reality. Among the many educators and people with whom Myles spoke was his former Professor Reinhold Niebuhr. He described his vision for the school in great detail to Professor Niebuhr. Both agreed that first a modest amount of money needed to be raised in order to start the school.

The professor, fully on board with Myles vision, decided to form an advisory committee who would sign a letter describing the principles of the new school. This allowed them to go out and solicit modest monetary contributions. A letter was drafted and sent on May 27, 1932. The heading on the letter read:

THE SOUTHERN MOUNTAINS SCHOOL
Temporary Address: 52 Vanderbilt Avenue Room 410
New York City

Director: Myles F. Horton

The fundraising appeal for a modest sum to start the school was successful, and mainly was due to the stellar reputation of those who signed it. Aside from Professor Nieibuhr, other members of the advisory committee who signed in support were:

George S. Counts, Professor at Teachers College Columbia University who was one of the founders of the American Federation of Teachers.

Norman Thomas who ran for President of the United States on a socialist platform.

Sherwood Eddy the International President of the Y.M.C.A.

This fundraising letter raised the needed $3,000 from small contributions. It indicated that the money raised to create the new school would be used to rent or buy a small farm in an impoverished community in the mountains of Tennessee. No one would initially be paid or take a salary. Wood would be purchased to be made into furniture, and the rest would be used for books and food. The aim was to make the school self-supporting as soon as possible.

Once the initial funds were secured, Myles began to search for a site. He met Don West who had shared a similar dream of creating a new school. Don was a Southerner from the mountains of Georgia who had also been to Denmark, and saw first hand how the Folk Schools there operated. He had studied theology at Vanderbilt University. Myles and Don had much in common, and so they teamed up.

The two young men, Myles and Don, drove around Tennessee in Don's old car scouting a location for the new school. By good fortune one night they stayed at the Reverend Nightingale's home, and during their late night conversations they learned that Dr. Lillian Johnson, who had also been a student of John Dewey, owned a farm in Monteagle, and wished to retire from the small agricultural cooperative she had established there. Dr. Johnson was quite impressive. She was among the first women in the South to earn a Ph.D., and had served as a college president. When Myles and Don explained their intentions to start a school, Dr. Johnson agreed to rent her Monteagle place to them for one year to get started.

The school was named THE SOUTHERN MOUNTAINS SCHOOL; but soon thereafter Connie, Don's wife, came up with a name they all agreed was more appealing; and the name was changed to the HIGHLANDER SCHOOL. Myles and Don became co- directors of the school.

The school's mission was to "help educate rural and industrial leaders to a new social order, to remove the conditions which led to extreme poverty, and to enrich the indigenous cultural values of the mountain people".

Modest beginnings truly describe the start at Highlander. Only two teachers and one student lived in the house in Monteagle. During the first year of operations there was a residential program of short courses, weekend conferences, and extension work in the community. Many local people attended. The school was free, and open to everyone regardless of creed, color, or religion. In the segregated South this was unheard of.

The Highlander School received a tremendous lift with the arrival of Elizabeth Hawes and James Dombrowski in 1933. Elizabeth had been educated at Vassar, the Brookwood Labor College, and the John C.Campbell Folk School. James had fought in France, and had attended Emory University, University of California at Berkeley, Harvard, Columbia and the Union Theological Seminary. He was a professed "radical" who had been jailed in 1929 for supporting a strike in Elizabethton, Tennessee. Both Hawes and Dombrowski recognized the vision and leadership of Myles Horton, and came to the school with their organizational skills to help him organize and grow the school.

The first class in Highlander was a psychology class because one of the local residents decided that this would be of interest. Soon many members of the community started attending evening discussions of psychology. Then after looking at pictures taken in Europe, a class in cultural geography was born. After teachers and students witnessed a coal miner's strike, an economics course entered into the unstructured curriculum. A woman who played the piano started a music class, and music and poetry readings became an integral part of Highlander.

The school was very loosely organized, and beyond subjects such as mathematics, literature, poetry and sociology; the courses were flexible and oriented toward the students' wishes and needs; focusing on experiential learning, and would introduce new ideas on socialism and labor unions. The school would also promote anti segregation laws and practices. It fostered the formation of agricultural cooperatives, the support of workers' rights, and a platform for social community events.

There were only a total of 8 students in the first term of the resident program at HIghlander. The term consisted of terms of 6 to 8 weeks. The staff worked without pay. The teachers and students subsisted mainly on turnip greens and beans. As needs arose to buy more books, and pay for gas to travel, and other necessary expenses, the cash balance at Highlander dwindled. On May 1, 1933 the cash balance at Highlander was a meager $5.57.

A six week summer program in the summer of 1934 fared well. Tuition was $30, and most of the class were members of unions like the Amalgamated Clothing Workers of America, American Federation of Hosiery Workers, and the United Textile Workers. The course format was more flexible with only required courses in labor history, labor economics and sociology. The other courses previously offered were all optional.

When the CIO union came to the south in 1935, Highlander was the only place where they found useful contacts for their union organizing efforts. Such efforts were fraught with danger because many of the existing companies in the South were determined to do all possible to avoid union organizing. Despite this, within two years Highlander became the official CIO union training center for all of the South.

Many of the staff members at Highlander also spent time outside the school in outreach programs, and in union organizing. They also helped other schools which were funded by the unions to train union organizers. Highlander was heavily involved in the local community, and always espoused and overtly practiced non-segregation.

Jim Dombrowski went to a town named Allardt where he set up a work camp and recruited people from all walks of life. There were professors, college students, ministers and local town folk all who quarried for rocks to build an adjunct school there because Dr. Johnson threatened not to renew the lease in Monteagle. She had become disenchanted and thought Highlander was too radical. Later she relented and did renew the lease.

Myles and Don alternated going from Monteagle to Allardt, when suddenly Don decided he no longer wanted to make that trip, and really desired to set up a school of his own. Myles and Don had an amicable parting, and the $200 which was all of their assets was equally divided, and Myles became the sole director of Highlander.

Informal weekend conferences were held at the Highlander School which also attracted people from the community who were not enrolled. This created a bond between the school and the community which turned out to be a very valuable asset when the school was threatened.

A few months after Highlander was opened, the staff and students supported a strike at a local mining company. In retaliation, evidence suggests that the owners of the mine hired a person to dynamite the school. When this became known, the community responded, and there were ample volunteers from the community who, without pay, acted as security guards around the clock. The security guards thwarted the threat, and no attempt was made at that time to dynamite the school.

Initially the academic program at Highlander was largely unsuccessful. A winter residence program was designed and offered in the years 1933-1934. The tuition for the ten week program was $75 or the equivalent in farm products or labor. Only four students attended. The emphasis seemed to be much more conventional then Myles originally envisioned. There were textbooks and courses in economics, psychology, sociology, labor history, English, public speaking, dramatics, arts and music. Early on raising money and the finances of Highlander proved to be a real problem.. On October 1,1933 Highlander's cash balance was less than the paltry sum of $6.00.

Despite these challenges, the early success of Highlander seemed to be with the community and the support offered striking workers. In July of 1933 a spontaneous strike of wood cutting workers took place.

The workers were hired to provide three hundred cords of cut timber known as bugwood. A distillation process extracted alcohol and other products from the wood. At 75 cents per cord, which was the pay the Company offered the wood cutters, meant that for a ten hour day the worker received less than 75 cents. This meager wage offered by the company, Tennessee Products of Summerfield Tennessee, was less than half of what was paid previously for similar work. The wood cutters demanded $1.50 per cord, and when the Company refused they went out on strike.

When the workers gathered at Highlander they were organized into the Cumberland Mountain Workers League to bargain with the Company. Myles Horton helped write a constitution for the League.

In part, this constitution stated as its purpose, " To prevent wholesale destruction to our forests, and to better the working conditions of the community by raising wages". The workers soon learned that while they were being paid 75 cents to cut down trees, the United States government was paying more to sponsor a reforestation camp in the same Grundy county. They went on strike, and were supported in their efforts by Highlander. The strike was not initiated nor significantly influenced by Highlander; but it did enhance the reputation of the school as a friend of labor in the South.

Highlander's teachers and students took part in other strikes in 1933 and 1934. They took part in the losing battle against the Harriman Hosiery Mills near Knoxville Tennessee. Even though their efforts in organizing and joining picket lines proved unsuccessful in this particular strike against the Hosiery Mill, the reputation of Highlander as a friend of labor was growing.

Violence against union organizers and workers who went out on strike was a common occurrence in those early days of unions trying to organize in the South for better pay and working conditions. Highlander was in the forefront of this worker movement, and also at the front of the movement to fight segregation in the South. Although Myles Horton believed in non violent protest, his adversaries often used violence, and even murder to achieve their goals. But those at Highlander resisted all kinds of intimidation, without resorting to violence of any kind.

Life changed for Myles in 1935 when a well to do student named Zilphia Mae Johnson arrived on the scene. She was a pretty, well educated young woman from Paris, Arkansas who had won top awards as a vocalist and piano player in Arkansas. As soon as he saw her and got to know her, Myles fell in love. She was the daughter of Guy Johnson who owned a coal mine. Her nickname was Zilphia, and it was she, who when at Highlander, found a little known song *We Shall Overcome*. She started singing it often at Highlander, and soon popularized it as an anti-segregation protest song. In addition she led many popular musical programs which were well attended. Soon she became the wife and colleague of Myles Horton. They both lived and taught at Highlander, and brought up their two children there.

In 1937 Myles Horton, in addition to all his other responsibilities and endeavors, felt the need to help the exploited workers who were white, black and Indian in North and South Carolina. He organized Carolina's Textile Workers Organizing Committee. It was not easy. The black workers were very suspicious of a white man trying to help them. Initially they would not talk to Myles. But he persisted, and explained to them that he was fighting for all workers and that they were union members and part of his constituency. Finally he succeeded in gaining their trust which resulted in a 100% increase in wages for them at the textile mill in McCall, South Carolina.

Horton was one of the few Southerners who did not look at the color of a person's skin. Carl Rowan, an independent researcher, said that there were only seven Southern educators who actively and publicly opposed segregation. Myles and his friend, Morris Mitchell, from Georgia, were two of those seven courageous persons. They believed all men should be treated as equals, and lived and practiced their belief. In the book *South of Freedom* by Carl Rowan, it was his observation that there were only seven white educators in the South at that time who publicly had the courage to advocate social equality, and an end to segregation laws and practices.

Threats, intimidation and violence were not confined to one year or one group, and there was always real danger. For example in 1934 in Daisy Tennessee the CIO Food and Tobacco Workers organized a strike which was actively supported by the Highlander staff and students. A peaceful parade was planned on Washington's Birthday in which local people, their children and the marching band of the local school, participated in support of better wages, working conditions, and the freedom to organize. None of the marchers carried any weapons or firearms.

As the march progressed a hail of machine gun bullets were fired and many marchers, including children, were shot and injured. However, despite the shooting the march continued to the gates of the mill where the workers stood singing *We shall Overcome*. Their courage won the day, and the strike was settled and the owners did give in to some of the demands of the workers.

Myles had been very supportive of strike efforts, and had participated once again in a picket line. The company realized that his efforts in supporting the strike and trying to organize workers to unionize were extremely detrimental to their perceived interests. They got other companies to join their campaign to thwart Myles' efforts.

Another strike in 1933 supported by Horton, staff and students came to be known as "Bloody Wilder". The lengthy strike occurred when the owners, Fentress Coal & Coke Company of Nashville, Tennessee told the workers that they would only keep the mines open if the workers agreed to a 20% cut in their already meager wages. The workers refused, and went out on strike. The owners closed the mines.

There were many violent clashes between workers, labor organizers, and companies who opposed better pay and working conditions. Among the threats and intimidation tactics of companies, organizations and individuals it should be noted that murder was not excluded.

The fact is that Barney Graham, a leader of the CIO union, was actually murdered; despite the fact that the murder plot was uncovered by Myles Horton who reported it. Horton's disclosure, and warning went unheeded, and Graham was murdered. The culprit, a guard at the Company, went to trial, but in Court he was exonerated and acquitted. No one was ever held responsible for this brutal killing.

At the same time as the school was earning a reputation as a friend of labor; it became recognized as a potent voice against segregation in the South.

A black college professor, J.H. Daves, from Knoxville College was invited to speak at the school on economic and racial justice, and the necessity of close cooperation by and between white and black laborers. students, teachers, workers, and other members of the community, black and white, came and listened. Highlander held the first integrated workshop in 1944. The "white community" was outraged.

Late in the year of 1945 there was a strike in Daisy, Tennessee supported by the folks at Highlander. A march was organized for those sympathetic to the cause of the workers. Children marched alongside the school band together with workers and others who believed that their solidarity would persuade the owners to recognize their just demands for a living wage. The march was peaceful, and no one carried a single firearm. As they marched past the mill, machine gun bullets were sprayed into the middle of the marchers. A woman next to Myles was shot in the leg. The few policemen who originally were observers disappeared and were nowhere to be seen. Despite the shooting, the courage of Myles Horton and his colleagues triumphed. They locked arms and sang, but let it be clearly understood that they would not be moved despite the intimidation. Their act of courage won the day.

Early on Myles learned that his perception of the problems the local mountain people were experiencing every day could be different from the people's own perception of these very same problems. He became a learner as well a teacher. He described the "fire in his belly" to ameliorate the condition of his neighbors. One of the important lessons that Myles learned about his anger, and how he should conduct himself, is when he himself compared it to a fire.

"I had to turn my anger into a slow burning fire; instead of a consuming fire. You don't want the fire to go out-you never let it go out-and if it ever gets weak, you stoke it, but you don't want it to burn you up. It should be an omnipresent slow burning fire. At times it must flare up; but then it should be subdued to stay for the long haul until it is no longer needed".

One of the most successful literacy programs was launched by a teacher at Highlander. It encouraged a large part of the black population to want to learn to read and write. Many literacy programs in other places in the past failed because they were there to teach people to read and write; but did not know how to motivate the local populace to want to become literate. Not so at the "citizenship schools" which became one of the most successful literacy outreach programs initiated at Highlander.

The "citizenship schools" although started at Highlander by one of its teachers, was never a part of Highlander. However it became one of the most widespread places where local people taught other local people how to read and write. In 1957 this program started and was so successful that it soon became known as "citizenship schools".

It started with one Highlander teacher, Bernice Robinson, motivating a few local blacks to want to become iterate. Her program spread like wildfire because she unlocked the key of how to motivate people to want to read and write. Bernice was a black woman who herself had not graduated High School, but who did attend Highlander. Myles was quick to observe her passion, and despite her lack of formal education credentials, he encouraged her, and permitted her to become a teacher at Highlander who focused on literacy. There she learned about the desire of her neighbors to learn to read and write. These local people then enlisted other black people to become teachers. By 1961 there were about 400 such teachers who had taught 4000 people to read and write. The teachers were local uneducated folk, mostly black, who themselves had become motivated and had mastered the skill of reading and writing.

The citizenship schools became so popular that hundreds of thousands learned to read and write, and 80% of those students were able to pass "the literacy test". As the schools proliferated, Andrew Young was brought in to head the program. Later he became the Ambassador to the United Nations, and the Mayor of Atlanta.

Myles Horton and his Highlander School guessed right about two of the United States most important social movements: the labor movement in the 1930s-1940's, and the civil rights movement in the 1950s -1960's. Highlander, early on, was intimately involved in both.

The set of principles which came from Myles thinking, dialogue with mentors, teachers, students and ordinary folk in the mountains of Tennessee were actually carried out at Highlander's birth. The school would be located on a farm. Students and teachers,white and black, would live together and raise food, and the emphasis was always on community, and studying ways to encourage the students to think for themselves, and to solve problems in the community in which they lived.

The outreach of the modest Highlander School, and that of its founder and leader, Myles Horton, went far beyond the Cumberland Mountains of Tennessee. It reached across the nation, and indeed across the world. The civil rights movement in the United states which it spawned, was the most famous result of the seeds Highlander planted. Other seeds which Highlander cultivated such as the growing labor movement, literacy programs, and experiential education sprouted and continue to grow in the USA and in many nations around the globe.

VI

DEATH THREATS

REACTION TO HORTON'S defiance of segregation laws, his help in organizing labor, and his teaching at Highlander, quickly incurred death threats from the "white ruling class". This class had the law on their side which favored segregation and exploited workers at factories and mines.

At times the local community had to post guards at Highlander when threats were received that the school was to be dynamited. Many of these threats were merely designed to frighten those who opposed segregation and supported labor rights; but were not carried out. The companies who were afraid of unions, and the "white supremacists", were determined to do everything to "stop Horton", and that even included murder.

A few threats were successful. Some who favored equality for all people and "workers rights" were intimidated, and so did not act; but not so for those at Highlander who were committed and unafraid.

In a desperate attempt to silence his voice, a Company whose labor policies Horton opposed, hired four men to actually assassinate him. Myles learned about the plot and skillfully worked out a plan to thwart this attempt to kill him. He stayed in his room at a hotel, watching from his window where he could view the street and waited. He carried a gun, but had no intention of using it. His belief and commitment to nonviolence was deeply rooted and firm.

Myles saw the car with the four men park in front of the hotel. He opened the window, and said to the men," Hello, I am Myles Horton; I understand you were hired to kill me; with my only crime being that I am an organizer. As an organizer I suggest you organize as to who comes into my room first, who second, who third and who fourth. You should know", he said brandishing the gun in the window in easy sight of the men. "When you organize, be aware that the first two men who come into my room will be shot by me; it is true that the third man may be able to kill me; but not before I have killed two of you".

Horton was a mastermind in engaging his opponents to think. This tactic made the men realize that carrying out their mission could result in their own death. Horton successfully engaged them in conversation. The four would-be assassins suddenly became afraid, and rode out of town, aborting the job for which they were hired. Horton left the hotel unscathed, free to continue his organizing efforts.

This dangerous incident illuminated how Myles, time and again, had resourcefully used his intellect to defuse threats. Myles Horton had widely become known as a leader that championed workers' rights. In November of 1932, he first attempted to organize the workers of a local mining company. He was promptly arrested by the police as an agitator. His notes were confiscated but he was released unharmed. However, the owners closed down the mines due to workers protests and the violence that ensued.

In 1933 the mines reopened with armed guards hired by the owners who were using non-union workers to operate the mine. Horton learned of a plot to actually kill one of the strike leaders of the CIO union, named Barney Graham. He notified state officials of the plot; but they failed to heed his information and advice.

Myles started a publicity campaign to expose this threat. His campaign was dismissed by national guard officers who labeled him a communist, an agitator and accused him of being responsible for the continued violence. Actually Horton never supported or resorted to the use of violence. His efforts had turned to helping provide relief to the families of the striking workers. He worked with the Wilder Emergency Relief Committee, with the Fellowship of Reconciliation and the Church Emergency Relief Committee, to provide much needed food and clothing for the families of those workers who were out on strike.

Despite Horton's valiant efforts, strike leader, Barney Graham, was brutally killed in in a premeditated murder carried out by a company guard.

The *Chattanooga Times* used the phrase "Bloody Wilder", to describe the strike. The culprit and killer was a company guard at the mine named Jack "Shorty" Green. The evidence was strong, and so he was indicted; but the Court exonerated and acquitted him. To the dismay of Horton, the labor movement, and others, the investigation was quickly terminated, and no one was ever held accountable for plotting or executing the murder.

Eventually the strike was broken by the use of non-union workers and their armed guards. The ruthless exploitation and death threats continued against all who opposed workers rights or championed an end to segregation.

Threats and intimidation was part of a continuing pattern to silence the voices of those who opposed the injustice of segregation and the exploitation of workers in the South. Highlander's teachers, students, and colleagues were constantly targeted.

Such threats and killings did not start when Highlander was founded; nor did it disappear as a new century dawned. Long before

Highlander was a dream of Myles Horton, people of color were being killed. Not only were there individual lynchings; but the worst massacre in the dark history of race relations in the United States occurred on June 1, 1921 in Tulsa Oklahoma. Commonly known as the "Tulsa Race Massacre" or the "Black Wall Street Massacre"; 300 black people were killed and 800 were injured. More than 10,000 people of color were left homeless and millions of dollars of property was destroyed. In the Greenwood section of Tulsa a memorial monument was erected to commemorate this horrific massacre.

Later we recite the inexorable march, albeit much too slowly, to equality and to an end to racism in the United States. Highlander is still very much a part of this march.

The Highlander Research and Education Center still is a target for those who spew venom and hate. It not only dates back to the days when the school was founded; but continues in each decade.

As recently as March 29, 2019 an arsonist set fire to Highlander.

Another coat of paint easily removed the graffiti; but the fire, started by an unknown "white supremacist" arsonist, that engulfed the school in the Spring of 2019, is not that easily forgotten.

Not only were Highlander's building burned; but the unknown arsonist left symbols of hate such as Nazi swastikas, and signs of white supremacy, so that it was clear to everytone as to why the building was torched.

Highlander, its teachers, colleagues, and students were not intimidated, and the buildings destroyed by the fire were quickly rebuilt; and Highlander continues to this day on its mission to embody and disseminate the ideas of Myles Horton.

Just a year later, in 2020, the brutal killing of an unarmed black man, George Floyd, by a policeman, was witnessed around the world because the TV cameras recorded the eight minutes the policeman held his knee on George Floyd's neck during which time everyone heard Floyd screaming "I cannot breathe".

This incident ignited the embers of the civil rights movement and there were protest marches in 46 cities. The revitalized movement, "Black Lives Matter", has called for instant police reform and there is now hope that genuine reform will take place. Already some cities are enacting such reforms, and others are in the debating process as to what reform should take place in their police departments. Suggestions include a police department which is diverse, and reflects the race and ethnicity of the population they serve, a strict code on the use of firearms, the banning of assault rifles and magazines which are large and used in the military, a ban on choke holds, and a mandatory program of training and de escalation of extreme violent tactics. This provides a ray of hope; but clearly the United States has miles to go to eradicate the scourge of racism, and inequality.

VII

STATE OF TENNESSEE V. HIGHLANDER

DEFYING SEGREGATION LAWS, and becoming the focal point for union organizing, had always made Highlander a source to hate by some individuals, companies, and organizations such as the Klan who favored and wanted to protect segregation.

From the day Highlander opened it was oblivious to color. Black and white people sat alongside each other in the classroom, and shared their experiences and learned together. This was against the segregation laws which were embodied in the statutes of many states.

Many attempts were made to shut Highlander down and quiet the voice of Myles Horton. Individuals, companies, and organizations spewed hate and falsehood about the activities of the Highlander School, and they were often joined by officials of the State.

The state and officials of the government of Tennessee did little to hide their venom against Highlander; because it was a school which openly defied the segregation laws. Finally, when propaganda and public opinion failed to close Highlander, the State of Tennessee turned to the courts to uphold their segregation laws, and sued Highlander.

The first notable lawsuit was the trial in Blount County Tennessee in June 1963. It was held in the courthouse at Maryville, Tennessee. The presiding judges were Judge William Shields and Judge Asher Howard. The prosecutor was Attorney D.H. Rosier, and the courageous defense lawyer was attorney Edward F. Lynch who had a thriving local practice before he took on this case for the Defendant.

As soon as it was announced that he would represent the Defendant, the Highlander School, Attorney Lynch became a pariah in the town.

His practice all but closed down during the trial, even though he had shown his legal acumen by arguing the case for Highlander.

The lawsuit in Maryville Tennessee in 1963 revolved about alleged disorderly conduct and possession of liquor by some students of Highlander who were out on a camping trip. The local sheriff's office was notified of their whereabouts and sent his troopers to arrest them. The local troopers disregarded all the norms and legal procedures in making such an arrest. They had no search warrants and cornered the students on private property.

The troopers said they observed lewd behavior by and between white and black students, but were never able to prove this allegation. They then relied on a local statute prohibiting liquor to be used. Again the allegation was refuted. The trial lasted three days and the courtroom was jam packed with spectators. At the end of the trial the Court ruled in favor of the Plaintiffs.

The conviction was a foregone conclusion because despite the lack of proper police procedures, witnesses, and evidence; the Court was determined to rule in favor of the County to uphold segregation laws.

After the case was over; Attorney Lynch's entire client list evaporated, and sadly he had no alternative but to close his practice and move out of town.

This lawsuit was brought at a time when Southern leaders were in a battle against civil right activists. On June 11,1963 the Alabama Governor George Wallace, a staunch advocate of the segregation laws in his state, stood in the doorway at the University of Alabama to block the entrance of two black students from entering.

His defiance was widely televised throughout the country, and it was then that President John F. Kennedy, called it a moral issue, and ordered the National Guard to go to the University of Alabama to accompany those two black students into the school to register and become freshman. The National Guard under these orders from the President did their job, and the two students, protected by the soldiers, were admitted into the University without further incident.

Just 2 months later on August 28, 1963 about one quarter of a million people joined in a march on Washington D.C. And it was there that Dr. Martin Luther King delivered his inspired *"I HAVE A DREAM"* speech. In that speech Dr. King skillfully articulated how immoral and unjust segregation is, and how it is contrary to the perfect union that the founding fathers envisioned.

Threats, intimidation and violence were not confined to one year, one decade, or one group, and there was always real danger.

A strike in 1933 supported by Horton, staff, and students came to be known as "Bloody Wilder". The lengthy strike occurred when the owners, Fentress Coal & Coke Company of Nashville, Tennessee told the workers that they would only keep the mines open only if the workers agreed to a 20% cut in their already meager wages. The workers went out on strike. The owners closed the mines; but not before the brutal murder of the strike leader of the CIO union, Barncy Graham. Myles Horton learned of the plot to kill Barney Graham, and notified state officials of the plot; but they failed to heed his information and advice.

Despite Horton's best efforts, on April 30, 1933 the strike leader, Barney Graham, was actually murdered. The identity of the killer, a company guard, was known; but he was never punished.

The mines were reopened when armed guards, hired by the owners, accompanied non-union workers, appeared in large numbers to operate the mine. Horton had started a publicity campaign in which he exposed the threats to kill Barney Graham. His campaign was dismissed by national guard officers who labeled him a communist and an agitator who was responsible for the continued violence. Actually Horton was never responsible for any violence. His efforts had turned to helping provide relief to the families of the striking workers. He worked with the Wilder Emergency Relief Committee who with the Fellowship of Reconciliation and the Church Emergency Relief Committee provided much needed food and clothing for the families of those workers who were out on strike.

Much to the dismay of Horton, labor organizers, and unions around the country, no one was ever convicted for this flagrant brutal killing.

The *Chattanooga Times* used the phrase "Bloody Wilder, to describe the strike. The strike was broken by the use of non-union workers and their armed guards, and so the "ruthless exploitation of workers" continued, and violence and death threats continued and were not uncommon.

In 1934 in Daisy Tennessee the CIO Food and Tobacco Workers organized a strike which was actively supported by the Highlander staff and students. A peaceful parade was planned on Washington's Birthday in which local people, their children, and the marching band of the local school participated in support of better wages, working conditions, and the freedom to organize. None of the marchers carried any weapons or firearms. As the march progressed a hail of machine gun bullets were fired and many marchers, including children, were shot and injured.

However, despite the shooting, the march continued to the gates of the mill where the workers stood singing "We shall Overcome"; a song which became well known after Mrs. Horton was the first to start singing it at Highlander, and popularized it.

The worker's courage won the day, and the strike was settled and the owners did give in to some of the demands of the workers.

Myles' reaction was a sense of revulsion at the shooting of unarmed workers and their families, and the murders which took place without anyone being convicted or penalized. Mere revulsion, he knew was not enough, and so he continued his non violent activism to end the lack of justice.

He remained calm and said, "Highlander and the fight against injustice and segregation are ideas; you cannot padlock or destroy an idea".

The question of violence or non-violence, and obeying the law, seems easy to answer. For most people non violence is preferred, and certainly obeying the law seems the right thing to do.

However, on closer analysis the question is not so easily answered.

The analogy written by the Civil Rights leader, the Rev. Martin Luther King, from the jail cell in Birmingham in which he was incarcerated because he led the civil rights' march, is illuminating. He indicated that everything Hitler did in Nazi Germany was legal according to the horrific laws Hitler wrote; but the stance of the Hungarian Freedom Fighters in their violent struggle was illegal". One must look at the text, in the context in which it is written, to truly understand whether unjust laws should be challenged by non violent civil disobedience as was demonstrated by Mahatma Gandhi in India.

VIII

PALENQUE: BIRTHPLACE OF FREEDOM FROM SLAVERY

THE SMALL VILLAGE of San Basilio Palenque in Colombia, South America holds the unique distinction of being the first "FREE TOWN" in South or North America where former slaves became free, and set up a town where they could govern themselves.

Despite the large influx of tourists to the nearby beautiful seaside city of Cartagena, Colombia, including many USA college "spring breakers", and the many who come to witness the second largest bird aviary in the Americas, the road to Palenque, just an hour away, is one that is less traveled.

Indeed upon arriving in Palenque, after a one hour ride from Cartagena, there was little evidence of the historic nature of this place, and the reason why UNESCO recognized this town as a "Heritage of Humanity" site. The only inkling in the dirt unpaved village was a sculpture of a black man crying out, and breaking his chains. That and a hasty painted scrawl on the side of a building which read "Black Lives Matter" gave evidence that this town was still run by the descendants of former slaves.

It was the Portuguese, who saw how slavery was practiced by the various tribes and kingdoms in Africa. They quickly realized the riches such slaves could bring if they were transported to the New World. In 1526 the Portuguese brought the first African slaves to Brazil. It was not long after that other European nations started to engage in the slave trade, and Cartagena in Colombia became a main port destination.

If we had not run into a twenty four year old Peace Corp volunteer who was completing two years of service in Palenque, we would not have learned how Palenque became the first place where former slaves became free. He explained that he was the only white Peace Corp volunteer to reside here. He came from Los Angeles, California to help the local farmers increase their crop yield and earn a little more money. While in residence he studied the history of Palenque and during four hours he shared his insights and experiences in the town.

It was a common occurrence that slaves who were brought to Cartegna from Africa tried to escape their bondage. Each time the Spanish army, housed in the large hilltop fort overlooking the sea, set chase in order to capture runaway slaves; punish them, and return them to their former masters or put them up for auction.

One such slave, Domingo Benjos BIioho, with a small band of slaves outfoxed and outran the Spanish army. They first settled in the Serrania de San Jacinto mountains, and then when they were sure that the Spanish army had given up trying to capture them, they settled in Palenque; more than two hundred years before Colombia achieved independence from Spain.

The former slaves declared themselves free men, and formed the town to govern themselves. It is a unique place only 50 kilometers from Cartegna, with about 3500 residents; yet it has no police and no crime. Groups called "makuagro" watch out for each other and for the welfare of all the residents. It has its own language which is one of the 69 native tongues spoken in the country. The language is a form of creole with a mix of Portuguese, Spanish, and Bantu, a language from central Africa.

The town is still unpaved, but most houses do have electricity and running water. However, it is still the custom of most women to walk the dirt path to the creek to wash their clothes.

It is a place where the women wear colorful costumes, and music and dance is prevalent. Many men of Palenque play musical instruments; many of which they make themselves. A yearly festival in October features drums of all sizes and shapes.

Dance is also featured. The Batata school of dance is for students who are of elementary school age to teenagers. There are about 150 students of dance who attend the school each year which is housed in a blue concrete building. Most of the residents of Palenque love to dance.

One of the rather unusual boasts of the locals is that Palenque is so strong it bred a world champion fighter. The boxer who won the world title was affectionately called the "Pambele Kid. His real name was Antonio Cervantes, a resident of Palenque.

Today slavery seems a thing of the past; but not many can envsion the agony experienced by 12,000,000 slaves brought by sailing ship from Africa to the Carribean and the Americas. Think of just one sailing ship where in the bowels of the ship, in the hold, many black men and women were squeezed so tight there was no room to move.

The stench from those who died aboard the ship from malnutrition, and lack of hygiene or breathing space, was a commonplace occurrence aboard the "slave ships". Two million slaves died crossing the Atlantic in those sailing ships during voyages in the 16th to 19th century.

Portugal was the first European nation, in the year 1526 to transport kidnapped African black men and women to be sold at auction like a commodity to serve their masters to work on cotton, coffee, tobacco, sugar and rice plantations in "the new world". Other slaves worked in the gold and silver mines, and also cutting timber for shipbuilding, and as domestic servants.

It should be noted that slavery did not originate in the New World. Long before the Portugese brought the first Africans to the United States; many of the kingdoms of Africa were enriching themselves by conquering nearby neighbors, and taking as captors the inhabitants of the conquered tribes and using them, and selling them as slaves to other African countries and kingdoms.

In 1494 The Portuguese king had entered into agreements with the rulers of some West African states that allowed slave trade beetween their countries.This however, should not be misinterpreted to mean that Africans had any influence on the power structure. Power and riches in the new world were confined to capital companies and shipping and insurance firms in Europe and the New World who controlled and expanded the slave trade. Despite the fact that Africa provided the slaves for the Americas; there was no African tribe or country who had any influence or power in the "new world" which encompassed the Carribean and North and South America.

The first Africans kidnapped and brought to the new world were classified as "indentured servants". However, as the slave trade continued by the middle of the 17th century, African slaves and their offspring became the legal property of theIr owners, and as such were sold in the market like goods and commodities.

Soon the Spanish, the British, the French, the Dutch, the Americans, and even the Danes and Norwegians became slave traders.

Ii is estimated that only about 3% of the slave trade came from Africa in the 1500s. This figure rose to about 16% in the 17th century, and was more than 50% during the 18th century.

In 1807 the British Parliament banned the slave trade. One of the causes of the Civil War in the United States was whether the union could exist half slave and half free. But even after the war the slave trade continued.

Before the Civil war, the slave trade accounted for about 28% of the total number of slaves brought from Africa to the Americas. Almost a million slaves were transported in the 1820s alone, and this was part of about 3 ½ million slaves who sailed across the Atlantic in a fifty year span from1810 to 1860. Although many regions and kingdoms in Africa were active participants in the slave trade, West Central Africa consisting of the Congo and Angola supplied over 39% of those who were transported to become slaves.

Near the beginning of the 19th century some governments acted to ban the slave trade, and it took early into the 21st century for several governments to formally apologize for the transatlantic slave trade.

CRYING OUT FOR FREEDOM & BREAKING CHAINS OF SLAVERY
by unknown sculptor in Palenque, Colombia
Photo is of the Author and Photographer in the central square in Palenque.

IX

COURAGEOUS ROSA PARKS

IT IS GENERALLY recognized that Rosa Parks' refusal in December 1955 to go to the back of the bus was the spark that ignited the civil rights movement in the United States which was thrust forward by the Reverend Martin Luther King.

That spark would not have been there, had Rosa Parks and Martin Luther King not studied at Highlander. There they were taught the values of dignity, equality, and courage by the example set by their teacher Myles Horton.

It was he that supplied the embers in the tinder box for the fire soon to come. His quiet courage and non-violent acts in the face of much hatred from the citizens of the South who fervently believed that he was a renegade to thwart the laws of segregation; did much to inspire Parks and King in their quest to end the horror of segregation. He taught by example that each person is equal, and must be respected, and treated with dignity.

It was this sense of dignity which gave Rosa Parks the courage to refuse to move to the back of the bus, just months after she had been to Highlander.

Many people know Rosa Parks from the time in 1955 that she was arrested for not giving up her seat and going to the back of the bus as required by the segregation laws prevalent in the South. Not many people think of where Parks, and Dr. Martin Luther King, received their inspiration to stand up for civil rights.

Rosa Parks wrote, "I only knew that I was tired of being pushed around. I was a regular person, just as good as anybody else. There had been a few times in my life when I had been treated by white people like a regular person, so I knew what that felt like".

Rosa was born on February 4, 1913, in Tuskegee, Alabama. She was named after her maternal grandmother, Rose. Rosa Parks' parents, Leona Edwards and James McCauley were married in Mount Zion African Methodist Church on April 12, 1912. James was a carpenter and a builder, and Leona was a school teacher. Shortly after they were married, they moved to Tuskegee, Alabama which had a good reputation for supporting the education of blacks in black schools.

Rosa's parents had different ideas about their future. James wanted to travel, while Leona wanted to stay put in one house. Leona decided to move back to Pine Level, Alabama, when Rosa was two years old, to live with her parents and return to teaching. James lived with the family for a short period of time and then left to find work. It was Rosa Parks' mother who raised her.

Rosa did not see her father again until she was an adult and married.

Just like the Horton family, Rosa's family deeply valued education. Rosa's grandfather made sure that his daughter had an education. Her grandfather was born to a white plantation owner and a black slave. When his parents both passed away at a young age, he was unprotected and endured torture by the new white plantation owner. Given his upbringing, he had a hatred for white people and did not want his children to be at the mercy of others. He instilled the lesson that you don't put up with bad treatment from anyone. He enforced the importance of education because he saw it as a way out. Leona passed the same message to Rosa.

Leona taught Rosa to read at a very young age. She attended the one black school in Pine Level. The school was first grade to sixth grade. Rosa noticed the discrepancy between whites and blacks very early. The white schools were new and built with taxpayer money and the help of the county. Black schools had to be built with funds supplied by the people themselves, and they received no funding from the government to run the school.

White kids also got to use a bus to school and they went for nine months. Blacks had to walk to school and could only attend school for five months. The reason that the blacks had less time in school was that when spring rolled around, their families needed everyone to help with the harvesting. Such was the plight of the slave or "sharecropper".

Rosa remembered one time when she was very little that she was treated as an equal. A young northern soldier passed by Rosa's house and told Rosa, "what a cute child she was". At that moment she was treated like a young girl, not a young black girl and this stuck with her for the rest of her life.

In 1915, Rosa's parents, James and Leona McCauley, had their second child, Sylvester. Shortly after that, James and Leona separated.

When Rosa was 11, she moved to Montgomery, Alabama where she attended Miss White's school. It was a school taught by white women from the North who came south to educate black girls. Miss White had a very hard time in Montgomery; the school had been burned down twice. The staff remained confined to the school boundaries, and so had no connections with any other white people in the South.

Rosa had not just learned Math, Science, and English, but she learned, "I was a person with dignity and self-respect, and I should not set my sights lower than anybody else just because I was black. We were taught to be ambitious and to believe that we could do what we wanted in life". Rosa did not just learn these important lessons at school, she learned them at home, and Miss White reinforced that belief. Miss White's school eventually closed. Rosa's Parks, at a young age, encountered many incidents of white supremacy. She was bullied by white children of the same age, and called filthy names just because of the color of her skin.

Rosa attended Alabama State Teachers' College for Negros until the 11th grade when she was forced to leave Montgomery and tend to her dying grandmother, and soon after that her chronically ill mother.

Rosa first met Raymond Parks when a mutual friend introduced them. Raymond had just broken up with a young lady that the mutual friend knew. Rosa wasn't particularly interested in romantic experiences at the time because of some unhappy relationships. She initially was not attracted to Raymond because of how light his skin was. Raymond was in his late twenties and was working in a barbershop in downtown Montgomery.

Raymond was a determined young man and even though Rosa didn't show interest, he kept coming back to talk. They started going for rides to different places in Raymond's small red Nash. At the time it was very special for a black man to own a car and not be a chauffeur that was driving white people. Everyone called him Parks and Rosa enjoyed talking to him, "He was a nice man".

Parks was born on February 12, 1903, in Wedowee, Alabama. His parents were David Parks and Geri Culbertson Parks and they both died before Rosa and Raymond met.

In 1932, at 19, Rosa married Raymond Parks. He was a long time member of the NAACP (National Association for the Advancement of Colored People). He encouraged Rosa to continue her education to earn a high-school diploma; which she did the following year, and to join the NAACP.

In December of 1943, Rosa became the secretary of the NAACP. This is when Rosa officially became a Civil Rights activist. Later in that year, Rosa registered to vote and was denied. She tried a second time and was denied again. Finally, after two years her persistence was rewarded. In 1945, she received her certificate for voting.

In August 1955, Rosa Parks attended a workshop at Highlander on implementing school desegregation. This is where Rosa met Myles Horton and Dr. Martin Luther King Jr. Rosa arrived at Highlander in low spirits. Spending two weeks alongside 47 other students strategizing for school desegregation began to lift her spirits. "I was 42-years old and it was one of the few times in my life up to that point when I did not feel any hostility from white people", Parks said. She was in awe of Myles Horton and his calm non-violent fight against segregation and worker exploitation. She also greatly admired Septima Clark, who ran a workshop, and how calm and courageous she was. Clark had been fired from her job as a teacher because she had joined the NAACP.

Everyone admired Myles' continued courage despite the death threats and intimidation he received because of his anti-segregation views which were practiced at the Highlander School. It was he, more than anyone else, that instilled in Rosa Parks the dignity and self-respect that every human being deserves. He also taught her the courage to stand up for what is right.

A few months after leaving Highlander, on December 1, 1955, a historic date, Rosa Parks was asked to give up her seat to a white man on a Montgomery bus and to move to the back of the bus. She refused, and in a polite but dignified and defiant way said she would not move to the back of the bus. She was arrested by the police and stood trial and was found guilty, Her defiant refusal to move to the back of the bus, however, was the beginning of the Civil Rights Movement in the USA.

At about that time she had started work at the Montgomery Fair Department Store, but by 1956 she was fired from that job because of her Civil Rights activism.

On November 13, 1956, the United States Supreme Court ordered the State of Alabama to desegregate all public buses. This ruling upheld a lower court ruling in Browder v. Gayle that stated, "the enforced segregation of black and white passengers on motor buses operating in the City of Montgomery violates the Constitution and laws of the United States, and violated the Fourteenth Amendment's guarantee of equal protection under the laws". In response to Mrs. Parks's arrest and others before her, Montgomery's black community launched a massive boycott demanding better treatment for black riders. As the boycott continued for months and months, organizers faced arrest, legal intimidation, and violent attacks.

In the midst of the boycott, on February 1, 1956, black civil rights lawyer Fred Gray filed a lawsuit challenging Montgomery bus segregation in federal district court. The suit extended the boycott fight to the courts as a strategic extension of the civil rights campaign. Browder v. Gayle presented the claims of four black women – Aurelia Browder, Claudette Colvin, Susie McDonald, and Mary Louise Smith – who had been discriminated against on Montgomery city buses. The named defendant, W.A. Gayle, was Mayor of Montgomery.

Soon after the Supreme Court announced its decision, Montgomery officials announced the integration of city buses. The bus boycott officially ended in December 1956, after more than a year of consistent and organized activism. Beyond Montgomery, the Browder v. Gayle ruling brought about essential changes in segregation on public transportation and laid the groundwork for much of the civil rights legislation that followed". It was a real joy for Rosa Parks to ride a bus on the day the US Supreme court issued its ruling.

In 1957, Rosa Parks moved to Detroit and continued her civil rights activism. In March of 1965, she was at the forefront of the protesters on the civil rights' march from Selma to Montgomery Alabama which was televised nationwide.

Later she began working for congressman John Conyers in Detroit. During the three years that she worked for the congressman, both her mother and father died.

Rosa parks continued her Civil Rights activism and attended the dedication of the Civil Rights Memorial, in Montgomery, Alabama.

She is nationally recognized as the spark that ignited the civil rights movement in the United States by a sculpture in her honor which was unveiled at the Smithsonian Institute in Washington DC in 1991.

In her autobiography, she recognizes the progress that has been made by people of color. She wrote, "There are no signs on public water fountains saying color or white". Racism in the United States still persists, but the evidence of progress, albeit much too slowly, is noted by how many black mayors, black governors, and black legislators who presently are in office or running for office.

A person of color occupied the highest office in the land. These are very good signs; but much more must be done to eradicate, once and for all, the systemic racism that sadly still persists in America.

Rosa Parks wrote, "Sometimes I do feel pretty sad about some of the events that have taken place recently. I try to keep hope alive anyway, but that's not always the easiest thing to do. I feel that it is better to teach or live equality and love than it would be to have hatred or prejudice".

Rosa Parks lived a courageous and meaningful life. She died on October 24, 2005, at the age of 92.

X

FATHER OF THE CIVIL RIGHTS MOVEMENT & THE TIMELINE

IT WAS MYLES Horton's friend, the educator, Dr. Morris Mitchell from Clarksville, Georgia, who first dubbed Horton," The father of the civil rights movement".

It was an apt name, for indeed it was Horton that planted the seeds that would sprout the civil rights movement in the USA. The impact he and Highlander had on the civil rights movement in the United States is well documented by the students who had come to Highlander; including the young Rosa Parks and Martin Luther King. Other civil rights leaders such as Fannie Lou Hamer, who was sterilized against her will, Andrew Young, head of the Southern Christian Leadership Conference, Stokley Carmichael, Leader of the Student Nonviolent Coordinating Committee, Ralph Bunch, U.S. Delegate to the United Nations, Senator Julian Bond were among attendees at Highlander.

Other famous people such as Eleanor Roosevelt, the wife of President Franklin Roosevelt, and so First Lady of the United States, attended Highlander. She was also a champion of civil rights.

All these leaders sat next to local folk, black and white, some who were uneducated and extremely poor; but all were welcomed, and treated equally with dignity and respect.

White and black people sat alongside each other and shared their experiences and learned together. This violated the segregation laws prevalent in the South, and so produced hatred and animosity from many Southerners. But Myles and the school he founded led by example. They remained undaunted, even in the face of death threats. They disobeyed these unjust laws, and preached equality.

Dr. Mitchell was also an educator from the South who shared Myles' views that segregation was immoral, and that the racial segregation laws should not be obeyed. They also shared the belief that experiential learning was a great tool in the arsenal of education which they both learned from the great educator John Dewey, when they both attended Columbia University Teachers College in New York City.

Dr. Mitchell applied experiential learning to college education and founded Friends World College in Westbury, Long Island, New York. where students studying outside the classroom and abroad could earn a Bachelor's degree.

Myles Horton preferred to remain in the South and founded the Highlander School in the mountains of Tennessee for the Appalachian community, and many of his students had not even graduated High School. His friend, Dr. Mitchell, who also opposed segregation, preferred to go North and start a college.

Myles and his wife, who was instrumental in popularizing the song *WE SHALL OVERCOME*, joined their colleagues and students at Highlander who fought segregation. The values they learned and taught was the "tinder box" which ignited the spark known as the civil rights movement in the USA.

The yearning to be free is embedded in the soul of human beings. Therefore, it is difficult to pinpoint the exact date of the beginning of the civil rights movement toward freedom and equality.

Many believe, however, that the modern civil rights movement began when courageous Rosa Parks refused to move to the back of the bus in 1955. The reason for her refusal is well known. It was because she, and Martin Luther King, attended the Highlander School where Myles Horton instilled in them a sense of dignity, equality, justice, and courage. Many, therefore, concur that the moniker "Father of the Civil Rights Movement" rightly belongs to Myles Horton.

Below is a timeline of important incidents in the modern civil rights march to change the laws and attitude of Americans in order to protect, under our Constitution, every citizens' equal rights regardless of color, race, sex, religion or natural origin.

You will note that we thought it important to report the following two incidents which occurred before December 1, 1955 when Rosa Parks' courageous stand electrified a nation.

The first occurred on July 26,1948 when President President Harry S. Truman, himself a former army captain in the US Army, issued an executive order #9981 to end segregation in the Armed Forces.

The second was the landmark decision when the United States Supreme Court consolidated many cases and ruled on May 17, 1954 in the case of BROWN vs. THE BOARD OF EDUCATION against allowing segregation in the public schools in the United States.

Chief Justice Earl Warren handed down this unanimous opinion, in this case of Brown against the Board Of Education in Topeka Kansas, that segregated public schools were unlawful in The United States, and so were barred from existing.

THE TIMELINE OF IMPORTANT EVENTS IN THE CIVIL RIGHTS MOVEMENT

<u>August 28.1955</u> Emmett Till, a 14 year old black youth from Chicago is brutally murdered in Mississippi for allegedly flirting with a white woman. His murderers are acquitted.

<u>December 1, 1955</u>. Rosa Parks refuses to give up her seat to a white man, and move to the back of the bus. This courageous act of defiance sparked what most consider the beginning of the activist civil rights movement in the USA.

<u>January 10,1957</u> Dr. Martin Luther King meets with sixty black pastors, and other civil rights leaders in Atlanta to map out a strategy of nonviolent protests against racial descrimination and segregation.

<u>September 4,1957</u> Nine black high school students, commonly now referred to as the "Little Rock Nine", are blocked from entering and integrating the all white Central High School in Little Rock, Arkansas. President Dwight Eisenhower sends federal troops to escort the black students into the school. They enter but are continually harrassed.

<u>September 9, 1957.</u> President Eisenhower signed the Civil Rights Act of 1957 which became a nationwide federal law to protect voter rights. It carries with it a penalty and prosecution of anyone who attempts to suppress anyone's right to vote.

<u>February 1,1960.</u> Four black college students, now known as the Greensboro Four, staged a "sit in" at a Greensboro, North Carolina, Woolworth lunch counter where only whites were served. Their courageous defiance sparks many other "sit-ins" around the segregated South.

November 14,1960 . Four federal marshals accompany little six year old Ruby Bridges into William Frantz Elementary School in New Orleans. She is the first black student to attempt to integrate the all white school system. Her action inspired the famous artist, Norman Rockwell, to commemorate her effort in the painting he created four years later which he titled "The Problem we All Live With".

1961 . This was the year in which white and black activists known as "Freedom Riders" took rides throughout the South to protest segregated bus terminals. They attempted to use "whites only" restrooms and lunch counters. Many of these Freedom Rides were marked by violent incidents where white segregationists beat up the Freedom Riders. However, these acts did bring national and international attention to the struggle and the march toward freedom and equality for black people in the United States.

June 11,1963. In a defiant televised stance Governor George Wallace stood in the doorway at the entrance to the University of Alabama to block two black students from registering. It was then that President John F. Kennedy acted decisively and quickly sending the National Guard in to escort the two students past the defiant Governor so that they could enter and become students at the University.

President Kennedy responded to this incident, not only by calling on the National Guard, but also addressing the nation in a televised speech, watched by most of the citizens in our country, in which he defined the civil rights struggle as a "moral issue; old as the Scriptures….and as clear as the American Constitution".

June 11, 1963, Only hours after President Kennedy's speech which was watched by most of the nation; the NAACP official, Medgar Evers was assassinated in Jackson, Mississippi. Many citizens of the United States were outraged.

August 28,1963 An unprecedented march of 250,000 people to the mall in Washington D.C. took place to protest segregation and inequality and to join the fight for freedom and job opportunities for the black community. It was well organized and non violent, and it was here that Dr. Martin Luther King first gave his eloquent famous, "*I HAVE A DREAM*" speech.

September 15, 1963 A bomb at the 16th Street Baptist Church in Birmingham, Alabama kills four young girls, and injures many others. Coming less than a month after the March to Washington and Reverend King's eloquent speech, the nation is dismayed and many furious protests are staged.

June 1964 Three civil rights workers were brutally murdered. James Chaney, Andrew Goodman and Michael Schwerner, the three idealistic Jewish young men, who were murdered by the Klan, had traveled from New York City to the deep South to join the campaign to encourage black people in Mississippi to register and vote. The F.B.I were joined by 400 US Navy sailors in search for the killers They found the bodies of the three dead burned white men in a swamp. Eighteen Knights of the Ku Klux Klan of Neshoba County were found to be the culprits of this heinous crime.

All eighteen Klan members were indicted, but only seven were convicted, and none received the death penalty. In 1988 a popular film *MISSISSIPPI BURNING*, based on this heinous crime, was produced and played in theatres throughout the nation.

July 2,1964 A historic and courageous act by President Lyndon Johnson took place when he signed into law the CIVIL RIGHTS LAW of 1964.

Many had doubted that President Johnson, himself a Southerner brought up amidst segregation laws, would sign the bill; but to his credit he knew that it was right and necessary. The bill provided prevention of employment descrimination due to race, color, sex, religion or national origin. Title VII of the Act established the Equal Employment Opportunity Commission (EEOC) to monitor and help to prevent workplace discrimination.

February 21,1965 The black controversial religious leader Malcolm X is assasinated by a member of Islam, the religion he promoted.

March 7,1965 A date remembered in infamy as "Bloody Sunday". Six hundred civil rights supporters join hands in a nonviolent march from Selma to Montgomery Alabama to protest black voter suppression. Local police with dogs brutally attacked the marchers. This bloody confrontation was seen on television and most of the nation is horrified. Later there is a court battle over the right of civil rights protestors to march.The Court allowed the march, and Martin Luther King who led the march reached Montgomery on March 25th with the eyes of the nation on this non violent protest.

August 6,1965 President Johnson signed the "Voting Rights Act of 1965" to prevent the use of literary or other tests as a voting requirement. It allows federal observers to monitor polling places, and federal examiners to review voter qualifications.

<u>April 4, 1968</u> Dr. Martin Luther King, the leader of the civil rights movement in the USA, is assassinated on the balcony of a hotel in Memphis, Tennessee. The nation is in shock, and mourns the death of this great civil right's leader who led many nonviolent protests, and articulated in many a speech the dream of a non segregated society and the worth of every individual. James Earl Ray is convicted of his murder in 1969.

<u>April 11, 1968</u> The Civil Rights Act of 1968 was signed into law by President Lyndon Johnson. Among its provisions it provides for equal housing opportunity regardless of race, religion or national origin.

This law in 1968 codified civil rights in the United States, but by no means ended the quest for civil rights, equal justice, an end to segregation, unequal opportunity, and the vast disparity between the very rich and the poor; and so our nation still has miles to go.

XI

KINDRED SPIRIT FROM BRAZIL

WHEN KINDRED SPIRITS meet a certain chemistry quickly develops by and between the two parties.

So it was when Paulo Freire, an unorthodox educator from Brazil, came to the United States in 1987 and met Myles Horton, a man whom he had admired for a long time from afar. The chemistry was almost instantaneous.

It was uncanny how much the two men had in common. Some say the two bearded men wearing glasses even looked alike. What is non controversial, however, is the common experiences and beliefs that both men shared.

Both were born to families in extreme poverty. Both rose, against all odds, to become college educated, and to understand that conventional education was not meeting the needs in their communities in Recife Brazil, nor in the mountains of Appalachia in Tennessee. Appalachia still houses many of the poorest communities in the USA. Recife, Brazil where Paulo was born and taught is in northeast Brazil, also has many very poor communities. It has the highest birth rate, shortest life expectancy rate, highest unemployment rate and lowest literacy rate in that country. The area was dominated by sugar estates where slave and peasant unpaid labor tended the fields. It was not unlike the area in Appalachia where the main crop was cotton, also tended by slave and peasant labor. The vast dichotomy between the very rich and the very poor is still quite evident in both areas.

Myles, who was 82 years old, was 16 years older than Paolo when they first met in July of 1987 at a conference in the United States. Myles had founded the Highlander School in 1932 in the mountains of Appalachia and remained there his entire life. Although through his writing, teaching, colleagues, and students, his ideas traveled throughout the world.

Paulo started his career, and was teaching literacy programs in Recife, Brazil in 1957. In 1963 he became the head of the National Literacy Program of the Brazilian Ministry of Education and Culture. Paulo, however, because of the political climate had to flee Brazil in 1964, and so continued his work in many countries around the globe.

Aside from being fascinated by Horton's ideas; there was a compelling thought which kept gnawing in Paolo's brain. It was that audiences constantly told him that his ideas were only applicable to third world countries. He knew otherwise, and wanted to demonstrate that these ideas were universal, and were on display in the richest and most developed country in the world as demonstrated in Tennessee in the USA.

Both Horton and Freire were teachers and learners and voracious readers during their entire lifetime. Paulo had read a great deal about Myles Horton, and had read all of his books. Paulo had also written books about his views on the need for education to change. Both men started their programs with rural workers who were being exploited. Industrialization in textile mills, mines, and factories were taking rural workers off the land; but exploitation and poverty persisted.

Both men received death threats and were jailed because of their unorthodox views which challenged the status quo. In both cases it was not only individuals and organizations who opposed their views, but the full weight of government, Paolo was exiled, and Myles had to defend himself in court.

Both men's first wives, who had closely collaborated with them and raised their children, died at a young age. Paulo Freire was terribly depressed when his wife, Elza, passed on; as was Myles Horton when his wife Ziphilia died. Later both men remarried, and again the similarities are unusual. Both men married young women who they knew, because both women had written their thesis using each man as their mentor.

Plaulo's second wife, Anna Maria Aranjo, had been one of Freire's students and wrote her thesis, under his guidance, on the history of literacy in Brazil.

Myle's second wife, Aimee Isrig, had worked at Highlander, and under Myle's guidance wrote her dissertation on the history of Highlander.

When the two men met they spoke about the books that helped them evolve their views. Myles spoke about the books of his great professors, and also how he had read the bible as a young man. Paulo mentioned several books, including all of Professor John Dewey's works, which shaped his thinking. Among other books which crystallized Freire's ideas on education were *Wretched of the Earth* by Frantz Fannon, *The Colonizer and the Colonized* by Albert Memmi and a book by the Russian Psychologist, Lev Vgotsky, *Thought and Language*.

After a discussion by both men about the aims of education, Paulo cajoled Myles into collaborating and to do a "talking book" together. He explained that in most books the author raises questions, but in their collaboration they would be asking each other questions and supplying answers from their own experiences. He said that just reading "the text did not supply the context".

The catch phrase Paulo used to convince Myles to do the "talking book" is when Paolo said of his constituents "I spoke to them, instead of speaking with them".

And so the collaboration was set for the *"Speak a Book"*. Paulo was to come to Highlander to spend as much time as necessary with Myles to complete the book which was to be titled *"WE MAKE THE ROAD BY WALKING" Conversations on Education and Social Change"*. The title of the book was taken from a poem by the Spanish poet Antonio Machado, which says," You Make The Way As You Go" This phrase epitomized Myles' thinking, so the book was to be "education in practice; both liberatory and participatory".

At their first meeting at Highlander, Myles said, "It's rather interesting that here we are within seventy-five miles of Ozone, over 60 years later from the time I was there, with the idea that really took form there; people learning from each other. You don't need to know the answer. You can help people get the answers…....These seeds were planted there".

Paolo responded with how much he liked being with Myles at Highlander. He also took the opportunity to talk about both of them being teachers, and that teachers world wide need to be more respected, and universally should receive a raise in salary. He also heartily agreed with Myles that good teachers also are learners, and that having people recognize their own perception of their problems and that their own experience is the basis of true education. Experiential learning is one meaningful path toward a real education,whether practiced in the United States, Brazil, or any other country.

Paola Freire and Myles Horton shared their experiences and life's journey in their "talking book" which Professor Jack Mezirow, at Teachers College of Columbia University called, "An indispensable book for anyone who still believes that ordinary men and women can be helped to learn to take control over their own destinies and to create a humane, democratic and just society".

Just three days before Myles Horton died, Paulo Freire visited him at Highlander where together they reviewed, and agreed on the final draft of their book.

The book began with the two men asking questions and providing answers.

Paulo asked," Myles who taught you to read". Myles replied that he really did not know. What he did know is that in the neighborhood he lived, there were no libraries or schools that had books. He had learned to read even before he went to school. Fortunately his parents kept a bible in the house, and so that was the first book he read. Thereafter the love of reading consumed him. He went house to house asking if they had any books he could borrow. "Luckily a distant cousin moved closer to where we lived. He was crippled; but his family were well to do farmers, and they had a bookcase which was filled with books;so I started reading from the first one on the shelf to the last. It never occurred to me that you had a choice and picked up this book over that book. I was just reading to read. To me it was a simple joy".

Myles' brother, Delmas, also liked to read; so the brothers took advantage of the Sears Roebuck catalogue offer that you could order 5 books for one dollar, and if you did not like the books you could return them and get a set of five new books. The two brothers, Myles and

Delmas, really milked the system by ordering, returning and reordering. They did this so often that eventually Sears Roebuck became wise, and refused to send them any more books.

Reading always was a pure joy for Myles, but it was not until High School that reading really made sense to Myles. He said," I started to understand not only the text; but the context as well, and I became more selective in my choices".

Paulo replied that it was his mother and father who taught him to read and write under the mango trees in his backyard. "I used to write with a twig in the dirt". Reading, however, at the time, was not Paolo's main concern, because in the 1920's times were very hard for Paolo and his family. He often went hungry, and that experience was paramount, and lasted with him for a lifetime.

When Paolo had to flee Brazil, he taught in many countries, and eventually wound up at Harvard University in Cambridge, Massachusetts. There he brought the concept of experiential learning, outside a classroom setting, more into focus. The Highlander School became an example. Its activities were well known because of Myles anti- segregation stance, and those of his students, who started the civil rights movement. Less known were Highlander's role as being a catalyst for the "citizenship schools", and literacy programs, and also for being a champion of helping to start to organize the labor and union movement in the Southern states.

When the subject of discussion turned to organizing labor and workers to join the fledgling CIO union in the South, Paulo asked Myles," are organizing and educating the same thing".

Myles was quick to distinguish the two by answering, "definitely not". Their goals are different. "Organizers are committed to achieving a limited specific goal, whether or not it leads to structural change or reinforces the system. You can see that this is very different from the goal of education". He then asked Paolo for his definition of education.

Paulo answered in expanding the role of an educator. The educator must have some knowledge, recognizing that this is forever changing." He or she must know in favor of whom and in favor of what he or she wants. It is dialectical, relating to the logical discussion of ideas. It works best when you can have the student begin and recognize all the things that the student already knows. His own experiences and that of other students studying with him is the place where a teacher must begin. Then it can logically progress in experiential learning, not necessarily in a classroom, where the student recognizes his own capabilities that can lead to structural change".

In winding up a good ending to their question and answer book, Myles recited a poem,

"Go to the people. Learn from them. Live with them. Love them. Start with what they know. Build with what they have. But the best of leaders know when the job is done, when the task is accomplished, the people will all say, we have done it ourselves."

Paulo heartily agreed, and was astonished to learn that the poem was written in 604 B.C by Lao Tzu."

XII

MYLES LEGACY: MILES TO GO

MYLES HORTON DIED of cancer in 1990 at the age of 85. In his waning years, even after he stepped down as the director of Highlander, he continued to teach, travel and hold workshops. He was working until the day he passed on. Just three days before he died, he met with Paulo Freire at Highlander in the mountains of Tennessee to finalize their book, *We Make the Road by Walking.*

His legacy lives on because of the values he instilled in his students and colleagues. He led by example, in a nonviolent way, the fight against injustice and inequality. He always said "the fight must go on, because we have miles to go". The path he set toward a brighter future for this nation is one that should be studied and followed.

Highlander, under Horton's stewardship, became more than the catalyst for labor and the civil rights movement. It became a learning and research center for justice and equality, and leadership in teaching individuals and organizations how to organize to fight effectively in a non violent way for their rights.

Whether it was fighting to outlaw segregation, eliminate poverty, worker exploitation and war, or strip mining, to protecting the environment from toxic waste and pollution, to adopting measures to promote literacy, to combating climate change, or to the remaking of some of our institutions dealing with elections where every persons' vote should count, and revising campaign procedures to disallow large money contributions; Horton's views and students were in the midst of the battle.

But make no mistake, the fight for true justice and equality is far from over; it has miles to go. As recently as 2020, killings and death threats continue to plague the African American community. In

Glynn County Georgia an unarmed 25 year old black man, Ahmaud Arbery, who was out jogging, was shot and killed. In the same year a target was placed at night in front of the door of the residence of the Rev.Keith Caldwell, President of the local Tennessee chapter of the NAACP, sending the clear message. Intimidation is part of the pattern of anonymous cowardly white supremacists.

In June 2020' an African American unarmed citizen, George Floyd, was murdered by a policeman in Minneapolis, Minnesota who had his knee on the neck of this unarmed United States citizen for a full 8 minutes. This was captured on worldwide television at the same time as the plea of Mr. Floyd was heard crying out "I can't breathe" before he died from asphyxiation. This brutal killing, after years of police shootings of black men and women, led to many weeks of continued demonstrations and marches, not only in 4300 cities in the USA; but also in many countries around the globe. It ignited the movement for structural change and real reform.

Many now hope that real structural police reform and accountability will now take place, so that there cannot be any more killing of individual unarmed African American men or women, or mass massacres like the 1921 Tulsa Oklahoma massacres which took place during Myles' lifetime.

The path against such brutality, segregation and inequality was set by Myles Horton, and despite the fact that the Highlander school was shut down by the State of Tennessee who revoked its charter in 1961; it was reopened the very next day under the name Highlander Education and Research Center where it has prospered to this day for 87 years since Horton founded the school.

In 1972 it moved onto 100 acres in Newmarket, Tennessee where it continues to focus on leadership training and organization skills and strategy to achieve social justice. Yet there are still those, including, but not limited to, "white supremists" who abhor the thought of social justice, and want to do anything they can to destroy Highlander and the values it espouses. Fascist graffiti is often found on Highlander's buildings in the morning, obviously placed there in the middle of the night by cowardly white supremacists. Threats to dynamite the school still circulate and an arsonist actually set fire to Highlander.

Despite such horrific acts, and continuous threats, Highlander was rebuilt and continues to operate using the same values espoused and lived by its founder. The legacy Myles Horton created at his Highlander School, and the example he set during his lifetime will long endure. The values he embraced, the causes which he supported, and the nonviolent good fight he fought, are embodied in the human spirit and enshrined in the constitution and principles of the founding fathers of the United States of America. Myles Horton, who led by example, showed us a path to follow.

However, there are still miles to go.

XIII

THE PATH

THE PATH TO a "great society" and a safe planet is clear to see. However the trek to get there has been diverted partly because this book is being written during two catastrophes.

The first catastrophe is the dark backward path initiated and implemented by an inept, immoral, President Donald Trump. It is good to illuminate this dark path in order to better understand how it has led our country into a divisive, violent, racist, poorer, future based on fear and disrespect for science, data, and truth; and to contrast this with the example set by Myles Horton. Horton's path which is actually the antithesis of such a dark path, is instead a shining path that Myles favored and practiced. It is a forward looking path based on truth, science, non- violence, an end to racism, inequality, and poverty which can only lead to a brighter future, and a more perfect union.

The second catastrophe is an unprecedented worldwide crisis caused by an invisible enemy known as the Coronavirus pandemic. This highly contagious, deadly unseen virus, which originated in China, has spread since the beginning of 2020, in a period of a few months, to almost every country around the globe. In the United States there are over 8 million cases reported, with a death toll in a few short months which exceeds 225,000, and unemployment claims exceeding 30 million people; and the numbers are rising each week.

There is a very high death rate in the USA from Coronavirus among the African American and Latino communities. This reflects the inequality which still is prevalent in these minority communities in this country. The death rate in some black and latino communities is about four times as high as in the white communities. The cause is quite evident. Because of poverty, many in these minority black and latino communities live in close proximity to one another, and so many cannot abide by the "social distance" and "lock down-stay at home" city and state orders. They have no savings and must go to work in order to feed their families. Also many are in the front line, working everyday in health care, exposing themself to the unseen virus which is rampant in nursing homes.

All agree that competent effective leadership is needed in every nation in order to contain the spread of this invisible killer virus. Unfortunately in the USA this is woefully lacking. Trump's lack of an effective response, and the absence of a national plan to fight the virus has led to a large portion of our population becoming infected and many of our citizens dying. Trump called Covid a hoax. Then predicted it would disappear by April 2020. His most ludicrous statement to the American people which he announced on national TV without consulting anyone is, "that citizens inject themselves with Clorox to ward off the coronavirus". This absurd idea was immediately rejected publicly by the entire medical and scientific community.

Objective scientists agree that the chaotic, unscientific response by the Trump administration to this unseen killer is responsible for these increased numbers of infections and deaths. Had a national competent scientific approach to contain this virus been instituted early in 2020, when the alarm was first sounded by the scientists, and when President Trump was advised of the danger of this pandemic; this very contagious virus, prevalent in almost every country in the world, could have been much better contained causing less infections and deaths in the USA .

It is noteworthy to observe President Trump's attitude at his political rallies where the wearing of masks and social distancing is conspicuously absent, and not practiced following the lead of President Trump. It is only one example which shows his complete disdain for science even though it was responsible for the death of his friend Herman Cain. This is the scenario of the rally, following Trump's advice and lead, in which the former Presidential candidate, Herman Cain, attended without wearing a mask, sitting very close to other people without the recommended six feet of social distancing. While there he was exposed to the Corona Virus which made him ill; and from which he died in the hospital.

Trump's modus operandi is never to admit a mistake; and not to learn from mistakes made. Trump is still holding campaign rallies where people, by design, are bunched together-there is no social distancing- and hardly anyone is wearing a mask. In a twist of fate, and sort of poetic justice, President Trump emerged from rallies where there were no masks or social distancing, and in October of 2020 President Trump himself became ill infected by the Covid 19 virus, and had to be taken to Walter Reed Hospital.

A good example of how the virus could have been contained is to look closely at what the Taiwanese epidemiologist who led the national effort accomplished in Taiwan, a country with a large population. He followed the science and instituted preventative national measures, including the wearing of masks, social distancing, testing and contact tracing. By using these well publicized public health measures he was able to keep the death rate in Taiwan to about less than 100 deaths in his country.

Many millions of people are unemployed because of the Coronavirus. The number of jobless people now even exceeds the number of unemployed workers in the USA during the 1929 depression.

The government in 2020 did pump an initial stimulus package of 3 trillion dollars into the economy; but as always many rich companies benefited; but the poor were still worrying if they could feed their family. Most economists agree that another stimulus package is very much needed. The House of Representatives led by Speaker Nancy Pelosi lobbied to have the $600 stimulus package renewed. The Republican led Senate refused to go along, and offered to cut the $600 to $300. As of this writing the two sides of the aisle are still at odds, and the new stimulus package remains in limbo despite the unspeakable suffering of the very poor who have no savings. The long and largest lines ever at food banks are unprecedented.

Because the flow of much needed funds from the government had stopped, some organizations started to give cash to those who otherwise would be hungry. A good example is the work that the National Domestic Workers Alliance did when the crisis became evident. They raised $35,000,000. Then, once a member of the Alliance completed an application, a debit card for $400 was immediately sent to the member so that much needed food or medicine could be bought. The process was monitored by the two consultants, Charley Wang and Matt Jorgensen, whom the Alliance had hired for various projects.

It is noteworthy that the inequality gap in the USA has grown wider; with less than 100 families having more wealth than if you combine all of the wealth of 90% of the USA population, and nothing, sadly, is addressing this inequality.

President Trump exaggerated and exacerbated this inequality, when he gave a permanent large tax cut to the wealthy, despite the fact that these billionaires were already paying a very much lower tax rate then they did under Republican President Dwight Eisenhower. This unneeded tax cut for the wealthy was done at the same time that the numbers of poor people in the United States, who have less than $400 in savings, and so have trouble feeding their families and buying their medicine, is growing at an astonishing rate, and is a real threat to the security of this country.

It is noteworthy to learn that despite President Trump's promise to release his tax returns; he hasn't done so. An investigation by the *New York Times* was published and revealed that because of questionable and illegal deductions, Donald Trump paid a total of a mere $750 in income tax in the years prior to becoming president. The reason for his refusal to share this fact with the American public is quite evident.

Due to an anachronistic presidential electoral system-the antiquainted electoral college- an incompetent President Donald Trump was elected, despite the fact that he lost the popular vote by millions of votes, and deprived a competent lawyer,and former Secretary of State, Hillary Clinton, from becoming President.

This is not the first time in recent history that the electoral college elected a president who lost the popular vote. Vice-President Al Gore, who demonstrated his competency and leadership qualities while serving with President Bill Clinton, also won the popular vote for the presidency, and was denied this high office by the electoral college vote, which was upheld on a partisan basis by the United States Supreme Court who intervened in the Florida election. George Bush who lost the popular vote became President, and Al Gore became a private citizen who has devoted his time to becoming the champion of the movement to effect the devastating effects of climate change. His motion picture film, *An Inconvenient Truth,* has been shown around the globe and documents in great detail the facts, and the present, dangerous threat to our entire planet posed by "climate change". President Trump calls "climate change a hoax".

To his credit our 43rd President George Bush did respond effectively to the threat posed by Islamist terrorists who destroyed the World Trade Center in New York City. True, many questioned President Bush's decision to wage war in Iraq and have troops enter Baghdad, despite the fact that his wise father, the former 41 st President Bush elected before him, forbade troops from entering Baghdad. Nonetheless, it is generally agreed that George Bush acted as a competent President uniting the country in the aftermath of the horrific act of destruction and loss of lives by the terrorist attack on the World Trade Center.

Not so with President Donald Trump, who instead of uniting the country, has by his rhetoric and "tweets" divided the country. His incompetence is now quite evident because he does not believe in science, and refuses to take advice from his own intelligence and scientific advisors. His former White House cabinet member, John Bolton, has written that, Trump" is ignorant and incompetent, and is not fit to be the President of the United States". Another cabinet member, General Mattis,concurred and uttered a similar remark at a different time. He said that " President Trump is not fit to be Commander in Chief and President of the United States".

Donald Trump's niece, Dr. Mary Trump, who grew up in the dysfunctional Trump household, is a clinical psychologist who claims President Trump has a mental defect known as a narcissistic personality disorder which craves adoration, and believes he is the smartest businessman and best President of all time. Nothing could be further from the truth. He went bankrupt four times, and had 3500 lawsuits before he became President. Eight of his closest advisors have been indicted. The Trump Foundation collected money but did not give to charity, and was closed after an investigation shed light on this scam. Trump University was a sham which took tuition from many unsuspecting people and was also shut down as a scam. President Trump on national TV mimicked a person with a disability, and also has publicly disparaged soldiers who died on the battlefield in defense of our country and values.

The mountain number of lies tweeted by President Trump is unprecedented, as are his broken promises. He promised as a candidate to release his tax returns as all Presidents before him have done. Instead he has been going to the courts to stop the release of his tax returns. To date he has lost every court battle, and the courts have ruled he must release those tax returns. To date he has not done so.

President Trump does not read the weekly intelligence briefings, and tends to fire any cabinet member who disagrees with him. The New York Times documented over 1000 blatant lies he has told the American people. The title of Mary Trump's book, "*TOO MUCH AND NEVER ENOUGH-HOW MY FAMILY CREATED THE WORLD'S MOST DANGEROUS MAN*", details how Donald Trump grew up in a highly dysfunctional household, evaded the draft, and became a favorite of his egoistic father, Fred Trump. Both Donald and his father were sued over discrimination for preventing black families from moving into their apartment houses.

Donald Trump has continued to side with the Russian dictator, Vladimir Putin, on every issue; even denying Russian involvement in the last Presidential election despite the unanimous assessment of "Russian Meddling" by every one of the intelligence agencies in our government. Thus his apt nickname "Putin's Puppet", and that of his

Senate cohort, "Moscow Mitch". Some speculate that the dictator, Putin, has some "dirt" on Trump so that Trump dances when Putin pulls the strings.

During the Coronavirus briefings President Donald Trump turned them into a political show. Showing his disdain for scientific advice he refused to wear a mask, and constantly derided the agencies which are there to protect the health of the populace. He has withdrawn from the World Health Organization, and did not even send a representative to the worldwide Coronavirus Vaccine Conference.

President Trump continued his policy of lies. *The New York Times* documented many of his deliberate public false tweets which he knew were just plain outright, blatant falsehoods. His "tweets", lies, and misinformation were a deliberate attempt to inflame his base of supporters, and his propaganda is intentionally divisive. Moreover he has tried to portray himself as the President who gives voice and is fighting for the working man. Nothing could be further from the truth as is evidenced by the fact that he refused to raise the minimum wage to $15 which the Democrats proposed, which would have put more much needed money into the pockets of working men and women.

President Trump "who knows more than anyone" continues to ignore science. In 2018 after the book *Fire and Fury* was published, Donald Trump himself tweeted that "he was a very stable genius." Stable and genius; those who know Trump know that the reverse is true; but that he craves adulation and self promotion. Rex Tillerson, the former head of Exxon, who Trump appointed as Secretary of State, soon learned that Trump was ignorant, and actually publicly called him a "moron".

Upon becoming President, he withdrew from the "Tokyo Climate Accord " which established a world wide protocol to reduce harmful pollutants into the air. This protocol which was initiated and led by President Barack Obama was signed by 197 nations. When President Trump took office he immediately withdrew from the historic agreement. The United States was alone with just one other country not to be part of this accord. Fortunately the other nations of the world remain in the Agreement in the hope that the next President of the United States will re enter and become part of this very necessary climate protocol.

This is not the only science, supported by more than 90% of the scientists in the world, that President Trump has called a hoax. In the United States President Trump has dismantled over one hundred environmental protection regulations, including but not limited to laws governing clean air and water; despite the horrendous finding of disease caused by high levels of lead in the 'brown drinking water" in Flint Michigan. He recently also did away with the regulation preventing high levels of mercury in our water even though such high levels have shown a direct correlation to brain cancer.

Indeed his mandate to the head of the Environmental Protection Department (EPA) was to dismantle all of Obama's regulations; in essence to dismantle the department . He seems intent on destroying all of the laws and regulations which President Barack Obama achieved,including the historic Affordable Health Care Act. He also abolished the Consumer Protection Department, and the Pandemic Response Initiative established by President Obama.

His status on the international stage has diminished the leadership role the United States has played successfully since World War II. Not only did Trump withdraw from the Tokyo Climate Accords, and the

Iran Nuclear Containment Treaty, but he withdrew from another treaty supported by almost every nation in the world. That treaty was largely written by the United Nations career diplomat, Eugene Wyzner, and provided that space would be free from weapons of war by any nation. Trump unilaterally, and without consulting anyone, established a new arm of our military called the Space Force. He has made it as important as the other branches of services equating it with the Army, Navy, Marine and Air Force. It's job is to create space weapons, thus thrusting other nations to also start developing such weapons of war, which if and when used, could cause irreversible damage to our planet, and to all the people of the world.

One way to possibly avert war is to implement an idea that Myles Horton supported when it was introduced as a bill for the US Congress to consider, which was initiated and delivered to Congress by Morris Mirchell's attorney, and sponsored by the U.S. Senator Vance Hartke. That is to have the President, The Secretary of Defense, The Secretary of State, all service personnel with the rank of General or Admiral, and all the members of the Congressional Foreign Relations Committee, take a mandatory course in CONFLICT RESOLUTION, DE ESCALATION & ARBITRATION at a U.S. Peace Academy; in the same way Army Generals take courses at the War College. The bill was never passed.

President Trump was impeached because he violated his oath of office for his own political motives. The House produced a transcript of his own phone call asking the President of Ukraine to interfere in our election process by publicizing an investigation of the Democratic nominee for President; former Vice-President Joe Biden. The second count of the impeachment is that he obstructed the Congress' House of Representatives constitutional duty of oversight by flagrantly not obeying their subpoenas. After receiving the evidence and Articles of Impeachment the U.S. Senate failed to convict President Trump because on a strictly partisan basis the Republican Senators voted not to allow witnesses to come forward and testify.

Contrast Donald Trump's actions with the path Myles Horton created. Horton's path is the exact opposite of the positions taken by the Trump administration. In addition to fighting segregation and worker exploitation, Myles has championed, and encouraged the many who have fought against many other unjust causes. Aside from his fight against segregation, worker exploitation and the ever widening disparity between rich and poor; he was an advocate for universal health care, a clean environment, and efforts to save our planet from destruction. He was particularly adamant about "public financing for elections", so that big money contributions could not sway the electorate.

Dr. Morris Mitchell said that Myles Horton was very vocal in supporting every citizens' right to vote, and strongly believed that each vote should be counted and that the majority of votes should elect all our government officials including the President. He abhorred voter suppression which still is unfortunately prevalent in policies set by the Trump administration. In 2020, before the election, Donald Trump threatened to severely cut the budget of the US Postal Service so that they would be unable to handle the millions of mail in ballots.

Redistricting is designed to favor a political party, and is not confined to one political party. Unfortunately both parties are guilty of gerrymandering.

An early advocate of "voting rights" was Congressman John Lewis who was one of the civil rights marchers bloodied in the early days of the civil rights movement. At his funeral, in July 2020, which President Trump did not attend or acknowledge, four former presidents came and paid their respect for this civil rights leader, and paid tribute to Lewis leadership in getting the voting rights act passed. During the eloquent eulogy delivered by President Obama, he delivered a stinging rebuke on the lack of leadership displayed by President Trump. Trump did not attend this funeral.

The courageous Senator McCain, who passed away, after witnessing Trump's slurs on his imprisonment during the war, specifically requested that President Trump should not be invited to attend his funeral, and Trump's absence was duly noted by leaders from around the world who did attend. Trump's remarks about service men and women who died whom he characterized as "losers" angered many.

An example of a recent more subtle maneuver to prevent many citizens from voting occurred as recently as. April 7, 2020. Efforts to suppress voting was quite evident during the unprecedented Corona Virus plague. Many states and governors were guilty of devising schemes to suppress the number of voters at election time.

The following is just one recent example. Because of the necessity for social distancing, the democratic Governor of the State of Wisconsin, issued an executive order postponing the primary election several months. This was opposed in the Court, which agreed with the Republican majority that the primary election could not be postponed. The primary elections were not postponed, but the world witnessed the suppression of voters despite the national law outlawing voter suppression.

In Milwaukee, Wisconsin during this 2020 primary election, only 8 voting places in this primary election were open, instead of the 85 voting places that is usual in that city; thus discouraging voting by many of its citizens.

Former President Obama who, after leaving office, was loathe to criticize Trump, found himself compelled to make a public statment which said President's Trump's incompetent response to the Coronavirus was "chaotic", and was the cause of many more infections and deaths in the United States.

The impeachment of President Trump was a "catch 22" impeachment, because Trump blocked the attempt to call witnesses, and then the Senate did not convict him because "of the lack of witnesses". A classic "catch 22" maneuver. His acquittal by the Senate is seen by many as an assault on our constitution because of the mountain of evidence of obstructing the Congress, and the treasonous act of having foreign countries interfere in our electoral process, was clearly presented by Congressman Adam Schiff, the Chairman of the Intelligence Committee of Congress. The Republican controlled Senate successfully thwarted every attempt to call witnesses, and obey subpoenas. Only one RepublicanSenator, Mitt Romney, who himself had been a presidential candidate, had the courage to speak out; the rest of the Republican Senators were silent.

Myles Horton was a staunch advocate of the disarmament of all nuclear bombs. He had read the essay Norman Cousins published fifty years ago in *The Saturday Review,* which was read by over 20 million people.It was titled *"Is Modern Man Obsolete",* and showed a chart detailing the number of bombs and their explosive power stockpiled in the silos of the United States and Russia at that time. Back then the total explosive power in the 2 countries totaled 15 Billion tons. Compare this with 3 Million tons of explosives which was the total explosive power dropped by the Allied powers during the entire six years of World War II. Then compare these true facts with the explosive power which exists today.

After the atomic bombs were dropped on Hiroshima and Nagasaki, a vast majority of the world's scientists declared that "100 million tons of explosive power might well turn the earth into a dark, frozen planet on which the extinction of human species could not be excluded." They called such a catastrophe a "Nuclear Winter".

Over 50 years ago there were only two nations that had many times more than the explosive power to destroy the world. Now with the proliferation of nations with nuclear arsenals, and the greater explosive power of the newer hydrogen bombs, the vast "overkill" capacity to destroy all living things on our planet has become a threat which the world should no longer ignore or tolerate.

At that time the nuclear bombs had much less explosive power then the ones today in the silos of the many nations that are considered "nuclear powers". Norman Cousins, the editor of *The Saturday Review*, accurately predicted the proliferation of "nuclear powers"; but even he could not comprehend the vast "overkill" explosive nuclear power existing today. Suffice it to say that Myles Horton believed that the leaders of nations vying to become nuclear powers, and those with nuclear bombs, do not really understand the amount of explosive power already existing today, and that there is a real threat of a "nuclear winter" wiping out all civilization on our planet.

Consider the facts: The first atomic bombs totally destroyed two cities in Japan, and left a horrific trail of radiation, and now hydrogen bombs are thousands of times more lethal. In 1954 the United States tested a 15 megaton Hydrogen bomb, and in 1961 the Russians tested a 50 megaton Hydrogen bomb which has 3,333 times the destructive power of the bomb dropped on Hiroshima. Is the world heading for disaster?

Among the 100 environmental protection laws and regulations which President Trump dismantled was The Clean Water Act despite the horrific amount of disease found in the brown toxic water in Flint Michigan. In April of 2020, as another example, the regulation which prevented the release of mercury and other toxic materials from being emitted by oil and coal fired power plants into our water supply was all but destroyed by the Trump administration; despite the fact that increased levels of Mercury has been linked in many studies to brain damage.

These are but some examples of the destruction of important laws and regulations that were opposed by Highlander students and teachers. It, therefore, is obvious that The United States of America still has miles to go to achieve the "perfect union" that the founders of our country envisioned, and which were so eloquently voiced by many of our great leaders.

The voices of our great Presidents, and competent leaders, among whom were Washington, Adams, Jefferson, Hamilton, Lincoln, Eisenhower, Truman, Kennedy, Johnson, Clinton,and Barack Obama still register; joined by the eloquence and courage of the assassinated leader of the civil rights movement, Dr. Martin Luther KIng.

Their example and "dream", and that of the example and dream of Myles Horton, the father of the civil rights movement, still echoes in the minds and hearts of many Americans.

Looking at the reality of the progress made in the civil rights movement which includes the historic achievement of electing a black President, and many distinguished black leaders of Congress, states and cities; make some believe that racism in the United States has vanished. Not so; a close look at the present state of our United States, and the recent killings of unarmed black people is proof that systemic racism still exists.

A hopeful sign is that 2020 is an election year, and perhaps the immoral, dangerous, authoritarian, untruthful, incompetent, chaotic,unscientific, divisive, rein of the Trump era can be put behind us;which surely will shorten the path to a "more perfect union".

XIV

MYLES TO GO

THE USA HAS *Myles to Go*; indeed it has many miles to go to realize the "more perfect union" the founders of our unique democracy envisioned. Yet the goodness, ability, and optimism of the American people to follow the right path and conquer any challenge remains the hope for our future, and for the future of the world in which we live, and the planet which we share. Let us all get started together to resume the journey for a better democratic unified country which again, by our example, can lead the world.

Courageous visionary Myles Horton blazed a path for us to follow.

# # #

SOURCES

Personal Interviews with Dr. Morris Mitchell, Clarksville, Georgia

Personal Interview with a Peace Corps volunteer in Palenque, Colombia, S.America.

Personal Interview with retired United Nations Diplomat from Poland, Hon. Eugene Wyzner

A & E Television Networks December 4, 2017 History: Civil Rights Movement Timeline

An Inconvenient Truth Motion Picture by Al Gore

Bill Moyers Television Interview of Myles Horton Google

Wikipedia

SELECTED BIBLIOGRAPHY

I Am Rosa Parks by James Haskins, Rosa Parks 1997

Moral Man and Immoral Society by Reinhold Niebuhr 1932 Charles Scribner & sons

Main Current in American Thought by Vernon L. Parrington 1987 University Oklahoma Press.

Quiet Strength:Faith,Hope and the Heart of a Woman Who Changed a Nation By Paris,Parks,Reed, J. Gregory 1994

Rosa Parks, My Story By Rosa Parks

Puffin Books,Penguin Group New York 192

Rosa Parks: My Story by James Haskins & Rosa Parks 1999

The Highlander,no ordinary school by John M. Glen, 1998 Kentucky University Press

The Long Haul by Myles Horton, 1990 Teachers College Press

Unearthing seeds of fire: *the idea of Highlander* by Frank Adams,1975 John F. Blair

We make the road by walking by Myles Horton & Paulo Freire 1990 Temple University Press

Who was Rosa Parks by Yona Zeldis McDonough

ABOUT THE AUTHORS

SPENCER GRIN, J.D. Ph.D. was the founder of *World Magazine* and publisher of *The Saturday Review* magazine whose readership reached more than 3 million readers. He also was President of the National Society for Arts and Literature, and on the Board of Directors of the American Museum of Immigration at the Statue of Liberty.

Spencer Grin, like Myles Horton, has fought throughout his life, for equal justice, protection of our environment and planet, and an end to racism and inequality in order to form a more perfect union; which alas, still has miles to go.

ASHER HEY, is a student at the Graland School in Denver, Colorado. He is on the Board of Directors of the Young Americans Bank where every person is treated with dignity and respect and given equal access and opportunity.

After he started research for this book; he was surprised to learn how few people knew who Myles Horton was, nor anything about how he planted the seeds of the civil rights movement, and fought for many good causes at The Highlander School which he founded. Asher's passion has been to shine a spotlight on the example set by Myles Horton, the Father of the Civil Rights Movement, and to illuminate the path he blazed for our nation and the world.

REVIEWS

"A must read about a remarkable man, Myles Horton, who was the inspiration for many civil right's leaders including Rosa Parks and Martin Luther King".

Deborah Shlian MD. MBA.
Award Winning Author and Literary Judge

"To better understand the problems facing the USA, and the path to some solutions; read this book. It details the life and work of Myles Horton, the Father of the Civil Rights Movement, and the educator who fought against segregation, worker exploitation, and many other unjust causes. It all started with his quest to help the impoverished communities in Appalachia."

Professor Judith Peck, Author, and Sculptor of " APPALACHIA"

Made in the USA
Monee, IL
30 January 2023

26767085R10080